AURA GARDEN GUIDES

Siegfried Stein

Water Gardens

AURA BOOKS

Aura Garden Guides

Water Gardens

Siegfried Stein

Original German language edition:
Gärten leicht und richtig
Wassergarten
© 1992 BLV Verlagsgesellschaft
mbH, München, Germany

This edition produced by:
Transedition Limited for
Aura Books, Bicester
and first published in 2002

English language edition
© 1995 Advanced Marketing (UK) Ltd.,
Bicester, England

English language translation by:
Andrew Shackleton for Translate-A-Book,
a division of Transedition Ltd.,
Oxford

Typesetting by:
Organ Graphic, Abingdon

10 9 8 7 6 5 4
Printed in Dubai

ISBN 1 901683 34 6

Photographic credits
All photographs by the author,
except:
Apel 28/29, 70 right, 71 left, 88/89;
Angermayer 85 bottom; Angermayer/
Pfletschinger 82, 83 bottom, 86, 87;
Bruce Coleman Limited/Hans
Reinhard 84; Burda 2/3, 18, 18/19,
19, 21, 30/31, 36/37, 37, 94/95;
Busek 49 left, 54/55; Eisenbeiss
28/29, 29, 49 right, 56 right, 65 left;
Neudorff 45; Pforr 22/23, 34/35, 35,
52/53, 55 bottom left, 64 left, 68 left,
83 top; Redeleit 46, 47; Reinhard 5, 7,
14/15, 55 right, 58, 60, 61, 68 centre
and right, 70 left, 78/79, 80, 81
bottom, 85 top; Riedmiller 54, 55 top
left; Sammer 6/7, 9 top, 12, 13 top,
26, 27, 38, 39, 50 right, 51, 89 left,
91; The Garden Picture Library (J S
Sira) frontcover

CONTENTS

The best position

Any garden can be improved by adding a pond: it's restful, it's attractive, and it allows you to look at nature in close-up. It can also provide a welcoming eco-system for endangered species of pond life.

If your main aim is nature conservation, you may prefer to put your pond in an isolated corner of the garden, well away from noise and disturbance. But there are also advantages in having it much closer to the house — perhaps even next to the patio — where you can watch things grow and develop. This should also put it closer to your water and power supplies, and will normally make it much more accessible when you're bringing in materials. This, in turn, will mean you can make better use of the site.

One vital element in the equation is the amount of direct sunlight your pond will receive at the height of summer. This determines the water temperature, which in turn has a deci-sive effect on the animal and plant life within it.

When choosing a site, try to avoid extremes of light and shade. In high summer the pond should ideally be in the sun for at least four to six hours a day. It's best not to have any trees too close to the pond: their leaves will pollute the water and alter the nutritional balance. In

This pond comes right up to the conservatory, so its attractions can be fully appreciated from indoors.

any case, if the pond is shaded, many plants (such as waterlilies) won't flower, or will develop too late. However, if there is no floating foliage to shade the water, it will eventually become much too warm for the animal life in the pond.

There are other factors to consider as well. You need paths or stepping stones that give access to your pond from at least one side (or preferably two). If it's close to a road (in a front garden, for instance), bear in mind that it will attract children — and that it could be dangerous. Small children have been known to drown even in a shallow pond only 8-12 inches (20-30 cm) deep. Putting a fence or railings around it isn't going to stop them. On the contrary, they'll be tempted to climb over it. A safer solution is to fix a sheet of strong, close-mesh wire netting immediately below the surface of the water, making sure that it's firmly supported from below. As an interim measure you could fill the pond with stones almost up to the surface (these could be removed later on).

Waterlilies and yellow flag need plenty of sunshine: they won't flower in the shade.

Pond dimensions

You'll find that the surface of a pond is soon covered by plants growing in increasing profusion. After just three or four years a single waterlily can occupy more than 20 sq ft (about 2 m²). The solution is to build the largest pond you possibly can, which is the only way to stop it filling up too quickly. If at least a third of the water surface remains free, you'll still be able to see the clouds reflected in it.

Practical experience suggests that a lined pond needs an area of at least 210 sq ft (20 m²) or 14 ft × 15 ft (5 × 4 m) if it's going to accommodate an interesting selection of plants. Preformed pools are usually smaller but they have steeper banks, which save space. On the other hand, you can always extend a lined pond if necessary, or add a second preformed pond.

You may decide to have fish in your pond. If so, you'll have to dig down to a depth of about 30 inches (80 cm). In hard winters the fish will need a protected area that can be guaranteed not to freeze over. Fish can also cause problems in a small pond, because their left-over food

Use earth dug out from your pond to make an embankment; it can be planted with a herbaceous border to provide shelter and create a favourable ecosystem.

often disturbs the ecological balance by affecting the nutrient content. Larger ponds can adjust to this more easily, and will also lose less oxygen during a prolonged heat wave.

If you're happy just to have plants, then your pond can be

much shallower. A depth of 4 inches (10 cm) near the bank and 36 inches (90 cm) in the middle is enough for nearly all winter-hardy water plants. Dwarf waterlilies will even grow in water 8–12 inches (20–30 cm) deep, but the current large-bloomed varieties prefer a depth of 24–36 inches (60–90 cm). Fortunately, such plants are hardly ever killed by the winter frosts.

It's easy to work out how much water there is in a pond, although this won't tell you very

Many kinds of fish like the cool water in the depths of the pond.

much about the general state of the pond life. Other factors — the surface area of the pond, the water temperature and the vegetation — will also play their part. But if you do know the water capacity (which is often indicated on a preformed pool), this can be very useful if you need to treat the pond with a chemical such as algicide (see page 88).

You can use some of the earth dug out from your pond to create a welcoming ecosystem for wildlife. Build a small embankment about 16–24 in (40–60 cm) high around the edge, leaving a large gap towards the south. This will give protection in many different ways. It will also look attractive if you cover it with stones and plants.

Matching the pond to the garden

A lined pond can be shaped to match your own special requirements. This is much the best solution for a do-it-yourself pond, or for a landscaped garden. Preformed ponds, too, come in many different designs, from round or angular to kidney-shaped. Among the most popular are ready-made 'natural' ponds: ponds formed into irregular shapes that mimic nature.

Tastes differ somewhat, but the recent trend towards things Mediterranean has brought a return to gardens in the classical style. Simple, clear lines are the order of the day, with pergolas, gazebos and rose arches. The pond must suit the style of the garden. A pool with straight edges is easier to combine with a patio, and also works well in a formal garden. It's also a better setting for displaying single plants. Straight edges are more restful than the wavy edges of a 'natural' pond, which start to look rather artificial when they're combined with the softer, more relaxed lines of a herbaceous border.

At one time preformed ponds had vertical edges. This made them dangerous for garden animals, and provided no accommodation for marginal plants. Nowadays they're provided with shallow margins, which are usually integral to the mould. Often they're specially roughened. This means that if an animal (e.g. a hedgehog) inadvertently slips into the water, it can get out without slithering helplessly into the depths.

Two former water-treatment ponds have been beautifully transformed to create a natural pond landscape.

Another idea is to install a combination of different pre-formed pools. Some manufacturers even provide a ready-made pond landscape.

If you're the do-it-yourself type, your natural choice will be a lined pond — and here the opportunities are endless. For example, you could extend an existing pond to create a marshy area. You could add a stream or an artificial spring, or even build in a waterfall. Or you could simply reshape the pond according to your own design.

 Clean the pond edges well and seal them. For a long-lasting, watertight seal use silicone or a good expansion bonding material. Real silicone (as opposed to cheaper substitutes) bonds stone with stone, and stone with lining. This means that there's no problem combining artificial and natural materials when you're building a garden pond.

Top *The gentle curves of this pond blend well with the planting around it.*

Right *Vegetation considerably softens the starkness of this square pond.*

9

Preformed ponds — the quick solution

Not so long ago most people preferred to build their own pond, usually out of hard-wearing concrete. However, since then the problems have become only too apparent. Concrete is expensive and awkward to work with. After a few winters cracks begin to form, and are very difficult to fill. A concrete pond also occupies a large area, which is often not available in a small garden. Finally, it takes a tremendous amount of effort to remove a concrete pond. Not surprisingly, then, such ponds have largely given way to lined or preformed ponds — and this despite misgivings and recent protests about the dangers of using artificial materials.

Most preformed pools are made from one of three main materials: polythene, ABS (acrylonitrile-butadiene-styrene) and glass-fibre-reinforced plastic, commonly known as fibreglass. Polythene and ABS are both light, flexible and easy to transport, and are best suited to small ponds. Fibreglass is usual for larger ponds, which need a stiffer, stronger material that doesn't buckle under pressure. Fibreglass is also appropriate for a unit construction system, in which several standard ponds are combined to create a whole landscape. The disadvantage of fibreglass is that it's heavy.

The pros and cons

It may be that you have limited space and want to create a really attractive water garden in a short time without having to work out all the proper ratios between surface area, depth and capacity. In this case the answer is a preformed pool. If the ground is steep or rocky, then a ready-made pond from a garden centre or builder's mer-

chant is again the best solution. You can even install a preformed pond on a patio or roof garden. You just need to use a little imagination to disguise the rather unconventional base material with a tasteful selection of plants.

Most preformed ponds are moulded in such a way that they provide shelves at various depths for plants with different requirements. Many pools even

Installing a preformed pool. Make sure it's level and the foundations are sound, or the water surface may appear to slope.

The ugly edges have been hidden under jute sacking planted with suitable vegetation.

include a shallow basin, about 6–8 inches (15–20 cm) deep, along the margins: this can form the basis of a boggy area. If you move house, you can take your pond with you: it's easy to empty, transport and refill.

The same pond after planting, complete with an artificial spring fed through a hose by a pump.

If possible, the edges of the pond should not be too smooth. A ridged surface allows any material that's floating in the water to settle — and any animals that fall in accidentally should be able to clamber out again without any difficulty.

All these extra refinements cost money. Preformed pools are rarely big enough to accommodate a lot of burgeoning vegetation over a long period.

On the other hand, you can always add another pond when your finances allow it. You could even add a lined extension. Try to hide the edges if you can: use a covering of stones and lush vegetation to keep them as natural-looking as possible.

 You can cover the edges of your pond with a long series of 'pockets' made out of jute sacking and sewn together. Anchor them to the edge, and fill them with rough, peaty soil. Plant them with suitable vegetation, and they'll improve the look of the pond no end. Whether it's a preformed pool or a lined pond, the edges will soon disappear. Eventually even the jute will no longer be visible.

11

Dig out the hole to the right shape.

Use a spirit level to check that the pond shell is level. Pack sand around it to make any necessary adjustments.

Installation

First mark out the perimeter of the pond with pegs, and dig out the correct hole. Measure all the dimensions carefully as you go, and do a trial installation before carrying on to the next stage. If the ground is hard or rocky, you should add a 4-inch (10-cm) layer of sand. This will cover any sharp stones that might puncture the shell once it's under pressure from the water filling the pond. If sand is hard to come by, you could use a suitable lining material. This normally takes the form of a roll of fleecy matting that can provide a long-lasting protective layer.

Before you finally install the pond, use a spirit level to check that it's absolutely level. If your pond is even slightly lopsided this will be a continual source of annoyance later on. As a final check, pour in about a quarter of the water you will need: you can still make slight adjustments at this stage if absolutely necessary.

Push plenty of really wet sand into all the gaps between the edge of the pond and the solid ground around it. This should prevent the pond shell from slipping sideways. After that, install the plants in baskets. When you've finished, add the rest of the water.

This plant can be installed at exactly the right depth by supporting the basket on a suitably sized block.

Even the smallest pond can look really beautiful. The plants along the edge make a pleasing transition to the rest of the garden.

Flexible pond liners

Most people these days use flexible pond liners to create their water garden — and with good reason. Pond liners are cheaper, and they can also be shaped to meet virtually all requirements. There's no limit to what you can do. A fish pond, a marsh, a stream — anything's possible with a pond liner.

A quality pond liner should be frostproof, durable and resistant to ultraviolet rays. It should not rot, and it should be elastic and resistant to pressure from growing roots. High-quality pool liners are often supplied with a guarantee lasting several years.

You must also choose a really stable material that doesn't leach out chemicals into the soil and thus contaminate the environment. Don't even think about any of the ordinary builder's lining materials. These will quickly decompose, creating an immediate hazard.

Even so there's a wide choice of good lining materials available. Most are black, but you can also choose blue, olive green or brown — whatever suits you. Dark colours give a greater feeling of depth, while lighter shades merge better with the surroundings.

There are many ways to achieve a natural effect. One method is to use a material that has a roughened rather than a smooth finish. This allows suspended matter in the water

to settle on the bed of the pond until it takes on a more natural colour. Eventually there'll be enough material for a little vegetation to become established. The other advantage is that animals such as frogs, newts and hedgehogs can get a better grip for climbing out of the pond.

Rubber liners aren't exactly cheap, but at least they are made of a natural material. They're elastic and durable.

Most pond liners are made of PVC (polyvinyl chloride), a stable, supple material that's hardly affected by light. PVC isn't exactly popular with conservationists, but research has shown that the base material of a pond has no effect on the kinds of plant and animal species that eventually colonise it.

One alternative is polythene. This material used to be vulnerable to light, and rather lacking in elasticity, but recent innovations in its manufacture have gone a long way towards solving these problems.

Liner measurements

You can buy liner material in various thicknesses. A thickness of about 0.5 mm is normally

There's no limit to the size of a lined pond, and you can lay it out in any way you like.

enough for a pond measuring up to 210 sq ft (20 m²), provided there's a layer of fleece or sand underneath to protect the liner from sharp stones.

Thicker liners (0.8 mm or 1 mm) are suitable for larger ponds, where the water pressure will be greater. These are more expensive; they're also heavier. A 0.8-mm liner will weigh nearly 2 lb/sq yd (about 1 kg/m²), so a larger pond will need a stronger team to build it!

Pond liners come in standard widths of four or six metres (13 or 20 ft), and in many other configurations: manufacturers can supply much larger sizes by bonding several sheets together, and the resulting joins are guaranteed leakproof.

Doing this yourself is hardly worth the effort. In theory it involves no more skill than repairing a bicycle inner tube with a suitable bonding material; in practice it's rather more tricky. First take the two pieces you're about to bond together (professionals don't talk about 'sticking' them together) and position them so that they just overlap. Paint the bonding material along both overlapping surfaces, and apply heavy pressure along the whole join (one way of doing this might be to drag a sandbag along it). The result will be a long-lasting bond. One word of warning — don't try this if the temperature's less than 60°F (15°C).

You need to plan your pond well in advance. Work out how much liner material you'll need, and allow two to three weeks for the supplier to deliver your order. Most manufacturers will bond sheets of liner together to create the pond size you need, and their bonding is fully guaranteed.

Bonding liner sheets together isn't really a job for the amateur, though it could be one way to extend an existing pond.

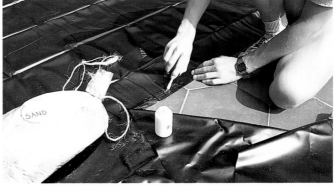

Creating the layout

First mark out the planned area of the pond with pegs, as for a preformed pool. Excavating the pond will mean digging down through a foot (30 cm) or so of topsoil to the subsoil underneath. Don't get rid of any of it. You can use it to redesign the surrounding garden and create some shelter for the pond. As the lower layers are generally poor in nutrients, they'll make an excellent substrate for water plants.

As you dig out the hole, don't forget that you'll need an extra 1-2 inches (3-5 cm) to accommodate the sand layer beneath the liner. This is vital to protect the liner from sharp stones. Any soil you put in the bottom of the pond will reduce its depth still further, so it may be realistic to dig out another 4 inches (10 cm) in all directions.

There are several points specific to lined ponds that you'll need to look out for. The underwater slopes want to be shallow, but at the same time you should incorporate a series of horizontal shelves. These will provide planting zones at depths of e.g. 4-8 inches (10-20 cm), 16 inches (40 cm) and deeper. This means you can safely install baskets of water plants at specific depths. Baskets on sloping ground might simply topple over and tip out their contents. Don't have any slopes greater than 45°, as the water pressure will tend to stretch the liner and

eventually weaken it. Even if you don't plan on keeping fish, it can still be an advantage to have a really thick layer of mud at the deepest point.

The edge of the pond must be at exactly the same height all the way round. This isn't easy to achieve: the ground will tend to settle, or it may get trampled down under people's feet. One way of tackling the problem involves laying flagstones with

> If you want your pond to include islands or small promontories, you should lay these at the right depth (10–12 in/ 25–30 cm) for planting close to the surface. Make sure they are big enough in area, and mould them into a depression surrounded by raised edges. Bear in mind that the liner will need to be completely hidden: it should not be exposed to sunlight.

rounded edges all around the pond, so you can pull the liner up over them later on. They'll also help to keep the edges at the proper height. For a smaller pond you can put pegs all around the perimeter, and use a spirit level mounted on a long, straight plank to transfer the correct level from peg to peg. For a larger pond you'll need an optical levelling device or a hose-type spirit level. This consists of a transparent hose half-

filled with water: if the water level inside runs parallel with the sides of the hose, then it is exactly level.

Work out the exact dimensions of the pond using a tape measure or a length of string and a ruler. Then you can use your measurements to estimate how much liner you're going to need. The formula should work out like this:

pond length (e.g. 4 m)	4 m
+ 2 × depth (e.g. 1 m)	2 m
+ 2 × edge width (50 cm)	1 m
liner length required	**7 m**
pond width (e.g. 3 m)	3 m
+ 2 × depth (e.g. 1 m)	2 m
+ 2 × edge width (50 cm)	1 m
liner width required	**6 m**

The edges will rarely need as much as the 50 cm extra given above. But it's better to have some liner left over (e.g. for lining a boggy area) than to find out that you need a lot more at the last minute.

It almost goes without saying that you should clear the whole area of any sharp stones, roots or other fragments. These can very easily puncture the liner when it's under pressure from the water. It's best to be on the safe side and fill the basin with a 1-inch (3-cm) layer of sand or fine gravel. If the ground is hard or stony, or if sand is hard to come by, you could use a roll of the fleecy underlay available at specialist outlets. A layer of plastic-covered wire netting below the liner will protect the pond against possible damage by voles.

If the ground is very steep or rocky, it may be advisable to create a smoother surface by laying a thin layer of concrete beforehand. This will further protect the liner from the effects of water pressure. The concrete doesn't need to be very thick, and doesn't require any base material as such. However, it does tend to break up rather quickly.

Try to find a team of helpers to help you lay out the liner. Smooth out any creases as much as you can, but don't be too fussy. The only problem is that the liner could split if somebody steps on a crease in winter, when the liner is brittle. On the other hand, any remaining creases can provide a hiding place for frogs and newts.

They'll also encourage floating material to settle, providing a good substrate for underwater vegetation.

Use stones around the edges of the liner to hold it in place temporarily. If you want a layer of soil to form the bed of your pond, use a low-nutrient mixture, preferably of sand and loam, that's free of any fertilisers or compost. However, a pond can usually manage without any soil: material floating in the water, including dead plant and animal matter, will gradually accumulate at the bottom. Finally, you can install all the water plants in their containers at the appropriate depths.

Now pour the water in very carefully. Stop briefly when the pond is just a quarter full to give yourself a chance to even things out. The water pressure will tend to press the liner into any irregularities in the ground layer

underneath. Start planting in the shallows before the pond is full, so the soil can settle around the plants. This is when the shelves and basins you've created will come into their own.

 The pond bed will look especially attractive if you tip a layer of round, white gravel over it, and around the planted areas in particular. The gravel will also prevent plants and soil from floating away.

The way you plant your water garden will depend on the way you laid out the pond in the first place. You need to plan a shallow zone for bog plants and a deep-water area for waterlilies.

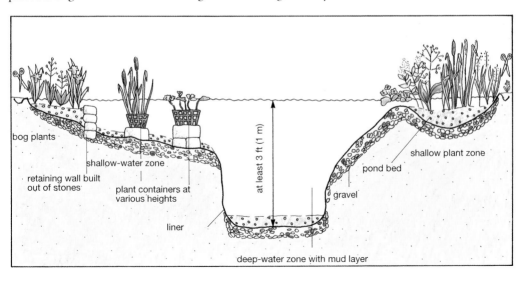

bog plants

shallow-water zone

retaining wall built out of stones

plant containers at various heights

at least 3 ft (1 m)

liner

deep-water zone with mud layer

gravel

pond bed

shallow plant zone

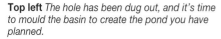

Top left *The hole has been dug out, and it's time to mould the basin to create the pond you have planned.*

Top right *The liner has been spread out over the pond basin. The rising water will gradually press it into the ground below. There's still time to smooth out some of the remaining creases.*

Above left *Plastic baskets are ideal for fast-growing water plants.*

Opposite page top left *If you want soil for the pond bed a loamy soil is suitable, but shouldn't be too rich in nutrients.*

Top far right *Crazy paving covers the edges of the liner perfectly.*

Right *As the plants bloom and grow in profusion, the full beauty of this water garden is revealed. The pond, and the animals living in it, become a pleasure to adults and children alike.*

The pond edge

As you've already seen from the illustrations, the edge of the pond is a vital element of any water garden, marking the transition between water and dry land. When you're deciding what to do with it, you'll need to choose between two radically different alternatives:

1 You can create a very gradual transition by bringing the liner all the way out into the surrounding vegetation. This produces a marginal zone — you'll often find something similar along river banks or lake shores. However, this wet zone absorbs water from the pond: the water level can drop as much as 2 inches (5–6 cm) a day. This 'wick effect' can be accentuated by the presence of soil, vegetation or even an overflow channel.

2 You can make the liner climb steeply at the edges. Once you've finished off the edges in the way you want, simply cut the liner back with scissors until it's no longer

 Your pond may look more natural if you create an overflow into the neighbouring vegetation, or into a boggy depression filled with plants that thrive in stagnant wet conditions. Make sure the boggy area is about 4 in (10 cm) lower than the edge of the pond. This prevents nutrient-rich water from seeping back into the pond.

visible. The marginal zone will be rather narrow, and the area outside the liner can be as dry as a bone. The advantage is that there's less evaporation, and the water level remains relatively stable. The only problem is that heavy rain could cause a flood. But you can prevent this by installing an overflow pipe running to the nearest drain, or to a gravel seepage basin.

There are many possible ways of hiding the liner.

Avoiding bare edges

Too much direct sunlight can damage the liner, but that isn't really the problem. It's simply that bare plastic edges are ugly to look at, especially if the water level drops. So what can you do about it?

One good method is to hide these edges under a skilful arrangement of ferns, overhanging grasses and herbaceous perennials. Creeping Jenny (*Lysimachia nummularia*) is a particularly good choice here.

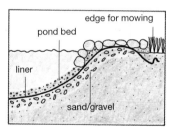

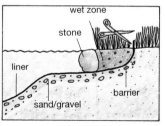

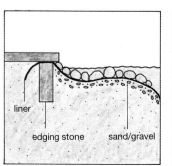

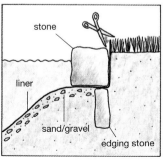

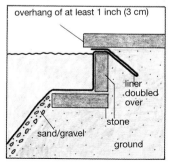

This ground-cover plant thrives in water as well as on dry land. It covers pond bed, liner and edges alike with a dense carpet of green, peppered with pretty yellow flowers. It will even grow on steeply sloping areas.

Gravel or attractive stones are only practical if the bank is shallow. If they are in danger of rolling off, a few drops of silicone on a clean liner may help put a stop to the problem. You could also lift off the turf from an adjoining lawn before digging out the pond, and replace it afterwards to cover the liner edges. In time this will form a very professional-looking transitional zone that you can mow just like the rest of the lawn — but be careful not to get lawn mowings in the water.

Pockets of jute sacking will hide ugly edges even if they're steeply banked. You can lay them down when you build the pond, or at any time afterwards. Fill them with soil, and plant them with suitable plants — it'll only be a year or two before they're covered in vegetation.

Other possibilities include paving stones (made of natural or artificial stone), wickerwork matting and wooden platforms. Bear in mind that anything made of wood (including railway sleepers) may leach out salts and oily substances, which at the very least pose a danger to fish.

The liner around the edge of this pond still looks ugly after several years, but jute sacking will soon put things right.

Clay and other materials

The first thing to say is that lined and preformed ponds are much easier and cheaper to install than any natural alternative. To build a clay pond, for example, you will need team of strong people who are used to dealing with large vehicles and heavy materials. The main problem is transport. If you want a steep-sided pond, or your garden is small, this natural alternative may pose insuperable difficulties.

Let's assume, however, that you've found a way around these problems — that there's a clay pit not far away, and that you don't have a problem getting hold of tractors and trailers. For centuries loam (minus any stones, which soon made it less waterproof) and clay were the usual materials for building fish ponds, or the water ponds used for putting out fires.

Make sure that your pit clay is free of impurities, and that it's moist and sticky, but not wet. Lay it evenly up to a thickness of 16–20 inches (40–50 cm). Now you'll need a road tamper to compress the material together so it doesn't crack.

When you've finished, add a thin layer of clay mud and smooth off the surface with a broom. On top of that put about 2–4 inches (5–10 cm) of gravel to provide a surface to walk on,

and finally lay the pond bed for the vegetation to grow in. The pond margins are more liable to dry out as a result of the wick effect, so in these areas it may be a good idea to include some pond liner in the clay.

Clay is a good building material for large ponds with broad margins. It's also a natural material.

Bentonite

This material is well known both to organic gardeners and canal builders alike. It's a kind of mineral clay that absorbs water and has strong binding properties. Because of these two characteristics it is used to make pelleted seeds, to seal clay pipes and to improve the water-retaining properties of sandy soils.

To build clay ponds you need heavy machinery and some strong workers to help you.

To make a pond with bentonite, you use a moulding machine to work it into the top 8–12 inches (20–30 cm) of the basin you have dug until it takes on the shape of a pond. You must add plenty of water, which the bentonite layer absorbs in order to become really firm. (This layer will always need a lot of water, which can pose a problem during periods of dry weather.) Then you smooth off the surface and line it with fleece before adding 4 inches (10 cm) of gravel. Finally lay down the pond bed, or put in water plants in baskets.

 With clay ponds you should install vigorously growing water plants in baskets so you can keep them under control. Take great care with phragmites and reedmace: if they're too close to the bottom, their suckers will puncture the clay and allow water to leak out.

23

Natural ponds and swimming pools

It's very rare to find a naturally occurring pond in your garden. For this to happen the water table must be high enough to fill the pond without any artificial assistance. However, such ponds, like naturally occurring streams, are subject to water and planning regulations, and you should bear this in mind when planning any changes or modifications.

Ponds like this rarely cause any problems as long as there's a continuous supply of water to keep them fresh. They also provide perfect conditions for keeping fish. Even ducks, swans or other waterfowl can live quite happily here.

Trout need running water in which to live. Carp and tench are also suited to medium-sized ponds or else situations where the water level varies. Fishing them out can be a troublesome procedure, however, so it may be an advantage to create some means of channelling water out of the system and guiding the

Above *A natural pond with lush vegetation goes well with a meadow full of flowers.*

Left *If the water table is high enough, then a pond may form naturally. Such a pond may be ideal for farming fish or waterfowl.*

Make sure that swimmers can get in and out of the pond safely. If you haven't got a sturdy ladder, then steps may be the best solution. Natural banks are often steep and slippery, making them dangerous for swimmers when climbing in or out. If nothing else will do, you should at least install a handrail for people to hold onto.

fish into their own special collection areas.

If you plant your natural pond with waterlilies, check for cold springs or water currents which can create problems for these plants. They prefer a warmer position near the bank.

The bigger the pond, the better its chances of remaining clear and healthy. During hot weather some people might want to bathe there. Even in an artificial pond, this is possible — as long as it's large enough. Ideally it should be about 5-6 ft

(150–180 cm) deep — 4 ft (120 cm) at the very least — and at least 20–25 ft (6–8 m) in diameter. Any vegetation should be confined to the banks or to underwater shelves. If you install plants in baskets, check they don't spread out too much, and cut them back if they do.

If your pond was originally built as a swimming pool, then it will still be very suitable for swimming even if it's planted with vegetation. It will probably have water purification equipment such as a pump and filter installed. But technology can be kept to a minimum, because floating plants, reeds and flowering rushes provide a natural means of purifying the water (see page 46).

You can still clearly see the shape of the original swimming pool. The very ordinary patio and pool have been transformed into a nature paradise.

Left *This large pond occupies a former vegetable garden. The deep-water zone is intended for swimming, and the shallow area for water plants that keep the pool clean.*

Below *The plants keep the water clear, so it's perfectly suitable for swimming.*

Water in a restricted space

Most gardens have only limited space, but this is no reason to do without water entirely. Small pools, preformed ponds, barrels and tubs hold only small amounts of water, which can easily get too warm to be suitable for animals. But there are no problems with plants in this respect.

A barrel, whether old or new, can make a very attractive container for water plants. You can even saw it in half to make two containers. It will provide space for a small water garden on a patio, in a courtyard, by the front door, or even on a balcony. Making it watertight is no problem, either: just fit a suitably sized pond liner.

You could also create a very effective display by placing a series of barrels together and planting them with an assortment of plants. A suitable combination might be zebra club-rush, common arrowhead, pickerel weed and water forget-me-not, each in a separate barrel. Some assortments might work better in a single barrel — for example, dwarf waterlily, mare's tail and water plantain with two or three *Mimulus* species in baskets.

Preformed ponds are well suited to small gardens. As most plants can manage in comparatively shallow water, your pond needn't be any deeper than 10–16 inches (25–40 cm). It will blend well into the garden, whether it's next to a path or among the herbaceous perennials. Such ponds can be round or irregular in shape — or they can be rectangular, to match the walls of the house. If you want to create a display with a really exotic flavour, choose some tender plants to join them

during the summer — arum lilies (*Zantedeschia*), water lettuce (*Pistia stratiotes*), papyrus (*Cyperus papyrus*) and water hyacinths (*Eichhornia*), for example.

A raised pond is no problem if you use a preformed pool, which is sturdy enough to be installed on a patio or even in a courtyard paved with tiles or concrete. Hide the outer shell of the pond with wood, planks or brickwork, and you can soon create a garden-like atmosphere.

An attractive bell fountain for birds complements this display of grasses and reeds.

A trough is most suitable in front of a building or on a patio. It can be made of wood or of natural or artificial stone. Possible water plants for the trough might include pickerel weed (*Pontederia cordata*) and dwarf waterlilies; these will also look good alongside a few tub plants.

Concrete rings can also be used to create small ponds. They look particularly good if you set them into sloping ground, or adjoining a stairway or patio. As they're normally used for laying pipes, you can buy them quite cheaply at a builder's merchant in various sizes up to 100 cm. You can place the rings one on top of another, and secure the joints with cement. If you want to ensure that the pool is safe, or if you just want to line it with a more colourful material, you

A stone trough can be converted into a well or a fountain.

can paint the inside with a waterproof paint. These paints are available in green, black, grey, brown or blue.

A patio pond won't take up much space. It can be sited right next to the house, dug into the sloping ground that is often found there. As such it makes a very good substitute for the old-fashioned rock garden.

An indoor water garden

Water plants from warmer climes make a beautifully exotic display during the summer — papyrus, lotus flowers, water hyacinths, water poppies and arum lilies, for example. The moment of truth comes before the first frost, when you have to find some place to overwinter them. At the very least, you will need a well-lit room that is frost-free — perhaps a conservatory, or an entrance stairway with plenty of light.

Many people are beginning to realise that a small water garden can greatly improve the quality of life in a home. If you set up a small water display with water plants, fish and imaginative lighting, the effect can be both charming and therapeutic. At the same time the water and the plants will improve the physical climate of the room.

Self-contained indoor fountains and bubblers are increasingly easy to find; they often have attractive design features and are available at reasonable prices. With a few rocks you can create a miniature waterfall within a very small area. Add a few tropical plants such as *Dieffenbachia*, *Spathiphyllum*, bromeliads and other epiphytes (clinging to stones or tree bark) and you can have your own miniature primeval forest. The sound of running water has a calming effect on many people, and gives the room an atmosphere all its own.

Most indoor rooms provide very little scope for a miniature pond, but a conservatory offers exactly the right conditions, with plenty of daylight, lots of space and a garden-like atmosphere. The plants you choose must, of course, be suited to the conditions, but if the temperatures are right you could choose a variety of species from tropical swamps or forest floors. You can grow them hydroponically or as pot plants, using natural stones, rocks, leca or cork bark where appropriate to create a beautifully exotic tropical display. You should put larger containers on castors so that they're easy to move around. Some of these may even be suitable for heavy troughs.

Left *A well-designed water display will look really good indoors.*

Right *A largish conservatory can be turned into a tropical haven.*

Vivaria and terraria

You may well want to include some suitable fish and amphibians in your water garden. By adding a few panes of glass you could even turn it into a kind of aquarium. This type of display is more accurately called a vivarium, as it isn't restricted to underwater animals. The marginal zone blends imperceptibly into a marshy area where frogs and newts splash around among the vegetation. Depending on the room temperature you could choose either native animals or species from tropical or subtropical countries. A vivarium thus provides the ideal place for watching the activities of small animals that live in or near the water.

Commercially available fish tanks come in capacities of up to 130 gallons (600 l), which is big enough to accommodate a small vivarium. If you want a larger size, you'll have to resort to DIY — although this should not pose too many problems. You'll need some panes of glass 6–8 mm thick, a frame made of metal or high-quality timber, and silicone to create a firm, lasting seal. Take advice from a glass specialist on the strength of glass needed to withstand the water pressure inside. The tank should be open across the top to allow for planting and cleaning, but if you're keeping animals in it you'll need a glass lid to stop them escaping. If you decide to keep fish you'll need an aquarium filter and a water pump.

A terrarium is generally a much larger structure that is open at the top. It's intended not so much for fish as for the animals that live around the margins, such as terrapins, snakes, frogs, newts and other amphibians. Whatever species you choose, they must be suited to life in captivity and able to live in harmony with each other. There should also be adequate space for their needs. The water will play only a secondary role, and even the plants themselves will be mainly for decoration.

The size and type of enclosure will depend on what animals you are planning to keep. A terrarium, like a vivarium, should normally have a base made of brick or reinforced concrete that's insulated from frost. The sides should be made of glass, plastic and/or wire mesh, depending on what is most suitable for observing the animals either in or out of the water. You need enough access to see to the animals' needs without giving them an opportunity to escape.

If you have species from more tropical regions, then it's essential to arrange some kind of heating, such as a low-power heating mat or an aquarium heater. One good solution might be a heating cable. This can be laid out all round the bottom of the enclosure, or stuck to the sides with heatproof adhesive tape, and is fully insulated by the manufacturer.

Terrapins need plenty of food and space.

A subtropical pond

If you want to breed tropical fish or amphibians from warm countries, it's actually possible to use an outdoor pond — as long as you can keep the water temperature high enough. However, even summer temperatures are scarcely warm enough, and spring and autumn are usually too cool, so these sensitive species invariably need an extra source of heat — use one of the various types of water heater listed above.

Water temperatures of 73–79°F (23–26°C) will provide suitable conditions for catfish, toothed carp and the pretty red-tailed tetra. They will also ensure a suitable environment for a variety of exotic water plants (see pages 74-77) — lotus flowers (*Nelumbo*) from Asia or North America, tropical waterlilies such as the blue-flowered *Nymphea daubenyana*, the sulphur-yellow water poppy (*Hydrocleys nymphoides*), the blue-flowered

water hyacinth (*Eichhornia crassipes*) and the water lettuce (*Pistia stratiotes*).

A similar structure, possibly supporting a foliage layer, might also prove useful for overwintering a number of beautiful bog

plants such as the lovely large-flowered marsh hibiscus (*Hibiscus moschatus*), the red-bloomed cardinal flower (*Lobelia cardinalis*), the white arum lily (*Zantedeschia aethiopica*) or Indian shot (*Canna indica*).

*A water hyacinth (*Eichhornia crassipes*) growing in a heated garden pond*

Fountains, streams and waterfalls

Once you have a pond in your garden, you'll be strongly tempted to extend it. Your first thought might be to provide some way of taking water in or out: the simplest solution is to install a pump and two pipes made of frost-resistant plastic. You could also sink a submersible pump into the pond bed, complete with a filter for cleaning the water. As a further refinement you could add a millstone, creating a gentle fountain that won't damage even large-leaved plants. If currents in the water are too strong, some plants such as waterlilies will not flower well, and may suffer from split leaves.

If you want to build a stream, you don't need to take out very much soil to create the necessary difference in height. In fact a drop of 3–5 ft (1–1.5 m) is all you need to create a gently flowing stream that falls in shallow steps. A bigger drop will require a stronger pump to bring the water back to the top, and cost more in both money and energy. A gentle stream looks more natural in a garden, and also blends more easily with the landscape.

You can also create a stream by installing a raised fountain. This can be fed through a hose from the existing pond, or laid out as a completely separate system. The simplest method is to install a submersible pump in the pond, or in a specially created basin, and use this to circulate the water. This kind of pump is relatively cheap, and can also be used for various kinds of fountains, sprays and filters. It runs quietly and will last for ever. A 60-watt machine will be quite enough to create a water column rising to about 4–5 ft (120–150 cm).

Vacuum pumps work on a different principle. They're installed in a pump shaft outside the pond, suck the water out of it, and pass it on. They are much more powerful — in fact they can often be unexpectedly so, emptying the pool with alarm-

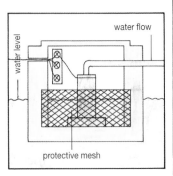

A vacuum pump needs a really solid pump shaft made of brick or concrete.

*This ambitiously planned stream is seen from above (**top**) and below (**left**). It runs in gentle steps from the patio down to the pond; from there it is pumped back up again using a submersible pump.*

ing speed. This makes them more suitable for a larger layout, and for faster-flowing streams and waterfalls. Such pumps rarely run quietly, and call for rather more effort and expertise to install. You need a pump shaft lined with brick or concrete to keep the pump dry and protect the suction chamber from contamination. There must also be plenty of air space around the pump to stop it getting too hot.

You can create a waterfall from preformed components (textured concrete can look surprisingly natural), or you could use rocks from natural sources. Their texture makes it easy for plants to cling to them, so they're ideal for indoor use. Many types of rock are perfectly suitable: they can be piled on top of each other or cemented into a waterproof base made of a flexible liner.

Water evaporates very quickly from waterfalls and cascades, so it's vital to install a system that adds extra water automatically. Otherwise you'll soon find that the pump is still running but the pond is already empty.

You can reduce water loss even further by using a barrier (i.e. extending the flexible liner over the surrounding soil). Flexible liners (similar to pond liners) form the best basis for creating a stream, because you can mould them to any shape you like. However, preformed components are also available in plastic, with a textured finish that will blend perfectly with the surrounding land.

A flexible liner will need to be hidden under gravel and pebbles. Incorporate a few small dams and waterfalls: this will allow you to develop some highly imaginative features such as bays and bog areas, which you can plant with bog or marginal vegetation. Marsh marigold, water forget-me-not, yellow flag, purple loosestrife, brooklime and rushes are all plants that feel at home here.

Calculate the width of the stream according to the water flow and the output of the pump. The water channel should be at least 6-8 in (15-20 cm) wide. You will need additional space for the stones and gravel that form the bank, and also for the vegetation zone.

Above *This miniature stream has been made from a length of flexible liner with a hose buried underneath it. A submersible pump has been installed in the bed of the pond.*

Below *A water feature made from a piece of hollowed-out tree-trunk*

Far right *A preformed pond with a fountain forms the source for a stream.*

Peatland plants

Peatland plants often look bizarre, but have a peculiar charm of their own. You may not be able to recreate the broad expanses of their natural habitat, but you can easily adapt any garden to create the ideal conditions for these plants. The soil must be poor in nutrients and highly acidic (pH under 5).

Peatland plants include many sensitive and therefore valuable species: marsh gentian (*Gentiana pneumonanthe*), sphagnum mosses, cross-leaved heath (*Erica tetralix*), bog rosemary (*Andromeda polifolia*), cranberry (*Vaccinium oxycoccos*), cotton grass, rushes and the so-called carnivorous sundews and bladderworts.

Make sure these plants never receive any nutrient-rich water from the garden pond or the neighbouring herbaceous borders, and never water them with hard water. However, you can plant them on an island in the middle of a pond or bog area. The planting zone should be at least 20–24 inches (50–60 cm) deep, and you should keep it totally separate from the rest of the garden. You can use any kind of deep container to do this — a concrete ring, a pond liner, a large plastic tub, a preformed pool or even an old bath.

Soft rainwater is ideal for peat beds, as it contains very little lime. It's simple enough to pipe it down from the roof guttering into the area where you want it. The best planting medium is pure, unfertilised peat that has been well saturated with water.

A display of this kind is only really attractive if it includes some patches of open water, a few tree stumps and one or two clods of peat to give the impression of genuine peatland.

Butterwort is good at catching flies.　*Cotton grass grows profusely.*

The marsh gentian is a particularly beautiful flower.

Insects are trapped by the sticky hairs of the sundew.

Nature and technology in harmony

When you first build a pond, you may want nothing more than a little piece of nature in your garden. But as time goes by you will probably want to create something more ambitious. This will usually involve some form of technical wizardry — pumps for water sprays, stones for fountains, lighting and cleaning filters. And the choice nowadays is extremely wide.

Water pumps today are amazingly robust, thoroughly sealed against water incursion and constructed to last a very long time. However, there are one or two points worth noting:

- Make sure your pump meets the requirements of the appropriate British Standard. This is the only way to be certain that an imported machine, for instance, conforms to the safety regulations governing these appliances in the UK.
- Make sure that all wires, plugs, lights and cables are properly insulated and protected from water, and get a fully qualified electrician to install them. Faulty connections quickly become lethal where water is involved. Take great care to ensure that all wires and pipes are thoroughly protected against the risk of accidental damage.

- Before you cover up the wiring, take a photograph to show exactly how it is laid out. This may provide vital information in the future, when you need to know how the pump is wired up.
- When you finally cover everything up, use large stones, tiles or piping to protect the wiring so that you don't inadvertently damage it with your spade.

A bell fountain creates no spray.

Fountain stones come in many different guises, and some offer surprisingly good value. You can take a large, attractive flat stone, drill a hole in the middle and install a submersible pump in a collecting basin underneath it. It takes very little pressure to make the water spray in all directions. You can find a suitable stone for yourself, but you should always get an expert to drill the hole — perhaps a specialist builder's merchant, or a stonemason who works on gravestones. This type of fountain is good by a pond, next to a patio, in a courtyard-type garden or even indoors.

Keep fountains away from waterlilies.

A **millstone fountain** works in a similar way, but needs a much larger basin for the water to circulate underneath. As genuine millstones are so cumbersome, many people these days prefer to buy a fibreglass imitation (suitably coloured and textured) — it's a lot easier to transport and to install.

Many gardens include **fountain sprays** made of terracotta or plastic. These come in a variety of different forms, some more tasteful than others. They include statues of people or animals that can be placed at the edge of a pond. Some will even float — useful if you need to install them in awkward or otherwise inaccessible positions.

Fountains aren't very appropriate for a pond that has been built to look natural. Animals don't really like the continually moving water, even if it does provide extra oxygen. Waterlilies, in particular, don't respond well if they are placed close to a water spray. The flowers often fail to open, reacting as if it were raining all the time.

On the other hand fountains are popular in formal ponds, fish ponds, and water features, including indoor installations. There is a wide choice of fountain systems on the market. Each includes a pump with variable output to produce fountains of different heights; a bowl to collect the water; and a spray nozzle, available in many different shapes and sizes. The possibilities are endless: you can have anything from an elegant ornamental display to a towering geyser. Depending on your taste, the rising water can take

A millstone fountain looks good in a modern or a formal garden.

the form of a water bell, a foaming plume or a complex water pirouette that changes over a period of several days.

Always install your pump on a firm base, and never directly onto the pond bed. This stops the mechanism getting dirty, leaves the water near the bed undisturbed, and keeps water movement to a minimum, which is good for the ecology of the pond. There are low-voltage pumps available that can even be powered by a 12-volt car battery.

Lighting, pumps and filters

Solar- and battery-powered systems have become popular for both pumps and lighting, partly because they don't need to be plugged into the mains. Besides being ecologically sound, this also means that the equipment is easy to install, even in the remotest corner of your garden. The amount of power available will depend on the amount of sunlight received and/or the particular system you choose. You'll need to ask a specialist about the systems that are currently available.

An oxygen pump

If you keep fish, it's advisable to have some way of oxygenating the water, just as you would in an aquarium. Strictly speaking a garden pond should be able to function without any help from technology. However, on hot days oxygen levels can become dangerously low, posing a threat to the fish within the pond.

To deal with such emergencies you need to install an aquarium pump in a dry position outside the pond (in a cellar, for example). Next you'll need a long plastic hose, and a few stones to disperse the oxygen. As the oxygen bubbles gradually rise to the surface, they are eagerly taken up by the fish in the pond. Oxygen pumps aren't particularly expensive, and they use only a small amount of electricity.

A filter system

For a pond to remain perfectly clear, its ecology must be in perfect equilibrium. However, there are many factors that are likely to disturb this equilibrium. There may be too many fish, or some of their food may remain uneaten; the pond may receive too much sunlight; or the depth and surface area may be in the wrong proportion. In all such cases a filter system will prove invaluable.

Basically, a filter consists of a low-power underwater pump that draws contaminated water through a series of membranes. These can be made from filter wool, plastic or a natural product of some kind (e.g. coconut fibre). The process removes all contaminants from the water. Periodically the filter must be removed and cleaned, then rinsed and replaced. The filter pump can also be used to feed a stream, a fountain or a water spray at the same time, or simply to mix the warm surface water of the pool with the cooler layers underneath.

There are many very reliable filter systems on the market, including some that operate according to the best ecological principles. See page 44 for information on purifying the water naturally.

Pond lighting

If you install underwater spotlights and a few coloured plastic filters, you can create a varied and highly original night-time display. However, overhead floodlighting alone will be quite enough to produce some remarkable effects in your water garden. The whole system should be well earthed and completely protected from water. Neon lighting should be shaded to prevent dazzle. Place the lights so that anyone looking at the display will always be standing behind them.

A suggested layout for a home-made filter system

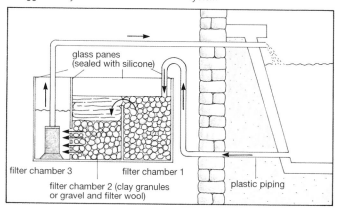

glass panes
(sealed with silicone)

filter chamber 3   filter chamber 1

filter chamber 2 (clay granules
or gravel and filter wool)

plastic piping

42

Some small animals only come out at night, and without lights you wouldn't normally see them. However, these same animals will obviously be disturbed by lighting effects such as floating balls, floodlights or underwater spotlights, which upset the natural rhythm of day and night. So don't turn on the lights, or keep them on, for any longer than you actually need them.

Floating plastic balls make the pond visible even at night.

Floodlighting can create a fairy-tale atmosphere in your water garden.

Water quality in your pond

If you're new to ponds and water gardens, you may well imagine that rain water is best for both fish and water plants. This assumes that you'll get a long spell of rain as soon as your pond is ready — which is rarely the case. In any case, rain water is generally too acidic for fish, and for most plants. As the atmosphere becomes increasingly polluted by industrial smoke and gases, the rain becomes polluted too. Sulphur dioxide is a particular problem: it dissolves in the rain to create a very dilute form of sulphuric acid (hence the term 'acid rain'). This means that rain water is rarely of sufficient quality. It's only suitable for a pond if it has been properly filtered first (through a bog area, for example).

River or stream water may be polluted with agricultural fertilisers. You will also need to get an official permit to use water from these sources. That leaves only spring water or tap water, which is, after all, clean enough for human consumption. Tap water is generally suitable for both plants and fish, although it often contains a lot of chlorine, which irritates the mucous membranes of fish. That's why it's best to let it stand in the pond to let the chlorine gas escape before you introduce any fish. In hot weather you'll only need to wait a few days,

but at other times you should leave it for several weeks. If that's too long, there are several products on the market that you can add to the pond water to make it safe for fish.

It takes only a few simple tests to determine the quality of the water in your pond. The most important factor you'll need to measure is the pH value (the acid–alkali balance), which should be somewhere between

6 and 8 (i.e. near neutral). You can raise the pH level by adding soluble lime to the water. You can lower the pH level by hanging sackfuls of peat in the water for a little while.

You should change the pond water as little as you can. Fresh water usually contains a fresh supply of nutrients, which disturbs the balance in the pond. Obviously you will have to clean it out now and again, but even then you should leave at least a third of the water in the pond. In the autumn pond life collects in the lower water layers, while

the overwintering water plants sink down to the bottom. In spring these remnants start to colonise the pond all over again. Even at other times of year the pond should never be emptied completely.

The simplest way to empty a pond is to run a hose from it to a point lower down. This will

A simple test is all that's needed to determine the pH value of the water in your pond.

The water quality in large ponds is usually self-regulating.

create a siphon effect: the water will flow along the hose provided that there's no air in it and the exit is far enough below the water level in the pond. Before putting the hose into the pond, fill it with water and hold your thumbs over either end to prevent any spillage. As soon as the pond starts to empty, put a sieve or a piece of porous cloth over the end of the hose that's in the pond. This will prevent any mud or solid matter from blocking it.

This method is very time-consuming, but it poses little danger to the life of the pond or to its environment. Another way to empty the pond might be to use a portable pump.

45

A natural water-purification plant

In some countries there are whole villages that have devised a biological method of purifying their waste water by passing it through a boggy area. Some private houses, camping sites, mountain huts, holiday cottages etc. have a similar system that makes use of plants such as reedmace (*Typha*), reed (*Phragmites*), flowering rush (*Butomus*) and bog rush (*Juncus*). In warmer countries even the beautiful blue water hyacinth (*Eichhornia*) is used for this purpose. Other suitable water plants are yellow flag (*Iris pseudacorus*), water plantain (*Alisma*), bur-reed (*Sparganium*) and arrowhead (*Sagittaria*) — but these are less effective.

First the waste water passes through a pre-purification plant (e.g. the three-chamber system). Next it flows down through a series of gravel beds filled with plants; these remove nitrates, phosphates and other noxious substances. It is known that some plants (such as the flowering rush) are even capable of breaking down complicated organic compounds.

If you have a suitable site with sloping terrain, this is one way you can improve the local ecology by natural methods. However, you must seek the help of a firm that's fully au fait with all the latest knowledge on the subject, and can guarantee to do the work correctly according to the relevant regulations.

The basic method is as follows. First dig a series of basins, each one lower than the previous one, and line them with pond liners. Then fill each basin with 1-2 ft (30-60 cm) of rough gravel, and plant them with reeds. The water filters down gradually through the series of basins into a pond filled with gently flowing water, where the cleaning process is completed. From here the water flows out to a sump, or is piped away for reuse.

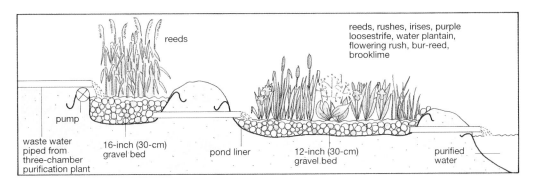

reeds

reeds, rushes, irises, purple
loosestrife, water plantain,
flowering rush, bur-reed,
brooklime

pump

waste water
piped from
three-chamber
purification plant

16-inch (30-cm)
gravel bed

pond liner

12-inch (30-cm)
gravel bed

purified
water

Left and below *The plants here provide a natural means of filtering and cleaning waste water. Natural purification plants are increasingly used for private houses, camping sites and even whole villages.*

Above *Cross-section through a natural water purification plant. The roots of various plants clean out the water as it is filtered through a series of gravel beds.*

The balance of nature

Undisturbed natural pools are filled with pure, clear water. Every pond owner wants to have water as clear as this — water free of brown and filamentous algae, so that fish and plants can thrive in it. This is rarely the case at the beginning. It takes time for a pond to achieve the kind of balance between growth and decay that's present in nature, and that keeps the nutrients in equilibrium.

Nutrients enter pond water in various ways: from the pond bed; from rain water that carries in dying remnants of the surrounding vegetation; and from the breakdown of dead plant and animal tissue during the autumn and winter months. Fish grub around and excrete further material. If fish food remains uneaten it sinks to the bottom, where it encourages the growth of bacteria and other tiny creatures that use up the oxygen. As a result, the nutrient levels in the pond will rise.

Water plants need some nutrients during the spring and summer, while they're growing, but if nutrient levels are too high algae start to appear, sometimes as early as April or May. The water becomes clouded by light-green or brown floating

In these flooded woodlands the natural balance is more or less undisturbed. Bog arum and water violet grow in profusion.

Blanketweed suffocates plant growth.

The water soldier uses up nutrients that might otherwise feed algae.

algae. In a newly built pond they will disappear just as soon as the pond clears naturally: in this case it would be quite wrong to replace the cloudy water with fresh, clear water.

However, if there are too many algae they make the water so murky that the underwater plants can no longer cope. They can't produce enough oxygen to break down the organic waste from plants and algae as it sinks to the bottom. The situation deteriorates until fish and other pond life are at risk. When the oxygen supply drops below a certain level, all life is suffocated. Bacteria multiply, feeding on the rotting organic material. The mud becomes evil-smelling and the pond gives off methane gas, which is poisonous to animals and plants alike.

An ecological balance is only possible if the nutrients coming into the pond are used up once they get there. There are several things you can do to ensure that this happens:

- Any soil for the pond bed should be poor in nutrients. Never use soil that contains fertilisers or high levels of humus.
- Keep the water soft and lime-free — i.e. keep the pH value down.
- Plant plenty of underwater vegetation.
- Don't feed the fish. If you do, you should feed them only very sparingly.
- Remove filamentous algae and dead vegetation.

49

The planting-out process

Now it's time to put theory into practice. Planting is a process that needs careful thought, but it also leaves plenty of room for the imagination. You need to choose suitable plants and group them so that their different colours complement one another in an attractive way. The aim is to create a harmonious combination. You also need to think about the pond's surroundings, including e.g. patios, paths, hedges and trees. Remember that from small, scattered beginnings the water plants will quickly grow into a sea of lush vegetation.

You may, for example, have been given some plants by neighbours whose ponds have already become too full. As they

A preformed pond often includes shelves for planting out marginal plants.

need to create some space they'll be happy to share some of their plants with you. The best time to do this is in the early spring.

Throughout the summer, gardening shops and garden centres offer a vast range of fine, hardy water plants. Many of them will be growing in baskets, so you can buy them in the middle of the flowering season and install them in your pond. They'll continue growing undisturbed. You can even plant out a pond in the autumn, when there's more time available than in the busy spring period. Besides, it's easier to get an accurate idea of the real amount of space that's available when your plants are in full leaf.

Many beautiful water plants grow naturally in the wild, but it's illegal to dig them up. On the other hand, nature can give

you plenty of good ideas about which plants you might include in your pond.

Your first job is to create a pond bed. You could use some of the lower layers from your pond excavations; alternatively you can buy something ready-made. Most water plants have shallow roots, so a fairly thin layer of 4-6 inches (10-15 cm) will be quite enough. If possible the soil should be gravelly, with a high mineral content and no fertilisers, manure or other organic compounds.

Line your planting baskets with plenty of jute sacking.

A border of stones will keep the water surface free; and it'll be a long time before these waterlilies in their basket are pushed out by marginal vegetation.

If the bottom of the pond is terraced or preformed with planting shelves, then there's no need to add any soil; you can put in your plants in plastic baskets. With some species (e.g. reedmace, bog bean and water-lilies) this can even be an advantage, because it makes it easier to keep their growth under control. Choose a basket that's large enough for the purpose and line it with a large piece of jute sacking. This should cover the whole surface area of the basket to prevent the soil and the plants inside it from floating, or being washed away.

When you buy water plants, carry them home in a plastic bag and protect them from sunlight until you plant them. Use unfertilised soil. If a root or any other part of the plant is damaged, cut it off to prevent the risk of rot. With container plants you can even take the opportunity to open up the firm root ball and trim the roots. This will tend to encourage new growth. Line the containers with sacking, press the plants down into them, and finally give them a good watering, prefer-ably *in situ*.

The pond will look more attractive if you then cover up the baskets — or even the whole planting surface — with a layer of gravel. This will help to prevent fish and other water creatures from stirring up the mud. Eventually the gravel will be covered by solid matter sink-ing to the bottom (which means, of course, that its attraction will be lost).

A selection of deep-water plants

Waterlilies

No pond is complete without a display of waterlilies. These plants produce glorious flowers that push up majestically between the leaves to create a magnificent display on the surface of the pond. They also create an ideal landing pad for dragonflies and frogs.

These plants include some completely hardy native species such as the white waterlily (*Nymphaea alba*) and the yellow pondlily (*Nuphar lutea*). However, both these species are strictly protected, and must never be picked or dug up from natural ponds. They only thrive in really deep water — around 4-5 ft (80-150 cm) — and will spread out over a considerable area, which makes them far from ideal for a garden pond.

On the other hand, various species have been crossed in cultivation to produce a wide range of cultivars that can be matched to ponds of virtually any depth. Most need very little care, and nearly all of them are hardy. The exceptions are a few copper-yellow varieties and the blue-flowered descendants of *Nymphaea × daubenyana*, which comes from warmer tropical waters.

Waterlilies spread out more vigorously if they're planted on the pond bed. Baskets tend to restrain their growth somewhat. A plant can occupy as much as 15-20 sq ft (1.5-2 m²) of the water surface within as little as two years. Waterlilies need plenty of sunshine in order to thrive, and they will not flower in the shade or if the water is too shallow.

If you plant waterlilies in baskets, there must be holes in the sides to allow the roots to spread. This forces the rhizomes to grow out sideways, so the tips will never be covered with soil. These plants grow faster in the warmer water near the surface, so start by putting them in the marginal zone at a depth of 8-12 inches (20-30 cm). Later on, you can move them

Nymphaea alba, our native waterlily, needs really deep water.

into deeper water, using an upturned pot or a brick to bring them to exactly the right depth. The best time for planting is between May and June, but you can install container plants at a later stage if you want.

Water plants don't generally need any feeding. However, waterlilies in baskets can exhaust their nutrient supply by the second or third year. If the leaves turn light green or yellow, or the flowers become too small, this is a sign that they need to be fed. You should

Recommended waterlilies *(Nymphaea)*

depth of water in inches (cm)	variety (cultivar)	flower colour
Dwarf waterlilies (small to medium flowers)		
4-8 (10-20)	*N. pygmea* 'Alba'	white
4-8 (10-20)	*N. pygmea* 'Helvola'	canary yellow
12-15 (30-38)	*N. laydekeri* 'Lilacea'	pink to lilac
15-18 (38-45)	'Ellisiana'	red
12-15 (30-38)	*N. laydekeri* 'Fulgens'	red to pink
15-18 (38-45)	'Aurora'	copper orange
Waterlilies with large flowers		
12-24 (30-60)	*N. candida*	white
30-72 (75-180)	*N. alba*	white
16-36 (40-90)	'Hermine'	white
24-32 (60-80)	*N. marliacea* 'Albida'	white
12-30 (30-75)	*N. odorata* 'Rosennymphe'	pink
16-32 (40-80)	'Mme Wilfron Gonnere'	pink
16-32 (40-80)	*N. candissima* 'Rosea'	pink
20-32 (50-80)	*N. marliacea* 'Rosea'	white to pink
20-32 (50-80)	*N. marliacea* 'Carnea'	carmine red
12-28 (30-70)	'James Brydon'	carmine red
24-32 (60-80)	'Gloriosa'	bright red
24-32 (60-80)	'Newton'	red
12-20 (30-50)	'Sioux'	copper yellow
24-40 (60-100)	'Marliacea Chromatella'	yellow
20-40 (50-100)	*N. odorata* 'Sulphurea'	yellow
39-60 (100-150)	*Nuphar lutea*, yellow pondlily	yellow
12-24 (30-60)	*Nymphaea × daubenyana*	light blue, tropical

confine yourself to using a special fertiliser that won't dissolve in the water or upset the nutrient balance. Fertilisers such as Liligro are designed to stimulate the roots into releasing the nutrients as and when they are needed. They're sold as sachets: all you have to do is press one sachet into the soil around the roots of each plant. There are also special waterlily fertilisers (e.g. Lilitabs) that come in the form of tablets.

53

Nymphaea odorata *'Rosennymphe'*

Nymphaea × daubenyana

Nymphaea 'James Brydon'

N. odorata 'Sulphurea'

Nuphar lutea, yellow pondlily

Other deep-water plants

This group includes some highly decorative plants — among them the pure-white water hawthorn (*Aponogeton distachyos*) and the golden-coloured water fringe (*Nymphoides peltata*).

Underwater plants are important to the ecological balance of a pond. Some float freely while others are anchored by thin shoots to the pond bed. In either case their leaves give off a large amount of oxygen into the water, even in winter (e.g. water violet, *Hottonia palustris*). They also help to discourage algae and provide shelter for young fish and other pond life. Some of them grow very profusely. Canadian pondweed (*Elodea canadensis*), for example, can be a nuisance, preventing other plants from reaching the surface. This tends to crowd out algae, but only by effectively taking over the whole pond.

Cuttings from many underwater plants will root if they are planted in a suitable growing medium. Floating plants are propagated by division.

The water chestnut (*Trapa natans*) produces edible fruit, while watercress leaves (*Nasturtium officinale*) are tasty and full of vitamins, making them an ideal ingredient for salads. A water garden can even be harvested!

*Golden club (*Orontium aquaticum*)*

*Water fringe (*Nymphoides peltata*)*

*Water hawthorn (*Aponogeton distachyos)

The most important deep-water plants (in order of flowering)

English name	botanical name	flowering period and position	depth of water in inches (cm)	flower colour, other remarks
golden club	*Orontium aquaticum*	May–June, sun	8–20 (20–50)	yellow and white, deep-rooting
water hawthorn	*Aponogeton distachyos*	May–June, sun	12–20 (30–50)	white and black, floating plant
water violet	*Hottonia palustris*	May–August, sun/half shade	12–24 (30–60)	pink to white, underwater plant, pretty flowers above water, graceful habit
water soldier	*Stratiotes aloides*	May–August, sun	16–32 (40–80)	white, floating plant, pretty shape, rosette-like, grows in groups
Canadian pondweed	*Elodea canadensis*	May–August	36 (90)	underwater plant, spreads profusely, oxygenating plant
frogbit	*Hydrocharis morsus-ranae*	June–August, sun	8–20 (20–50)	white, floating plant

57

*Water violet (*Hottonia palustris)

*Greater bladderwort (*Utricularia vulgaris)

*Water chestnut (*Trapa natans)

More plants for deep water or moderate depths

English name	botanical name	flowering period and position	depth of water in inches (cm)	flower colour, other remarks
floating pondweed	*Potamogeton natans*	May–August, sun/half shade	24–40 (60–100)	green, floating plant, underwater plant, valuable for young breeding fish, but regarded as a weed
starwort	*Callitriche palustris*	May–Sept., sun/half-shade	8–24 (20–60)	green, underwater plant, dense-growing evergreen
water crowfoot	*Ranunculus aquatilis*	June–July, sun	8–24 (20–60)	white, underwater plant, very pretty flowers, forms dense growth
hornwort	*Ceratophyllum demersum*	June–August, sun/half-shade	20–48 (50–120)	green, underwater plant, forms strong growth
whorled milfoil	*Myriophyllum spicatum*	June–August, sun	10–48 (25–120)	pinkish-green, underwater plant, needs lots of space, for larger ponds, though can be controlled in a smaller pond
greater bladderwort	*Utricularia vulgaris*	June–August, sun	10–32 (25–80)	yellow, floating plant, rootless, pretty flowers, bladders on leaves catch insects
yellow pondlily	*Nuphar lutea*	June–Sept. sun	40–60 (100–150)	yellow, floating plant, deep-rooting, only for larger ponds
Japanese pondlily	*Nuphar japonica*	July–August, sun	20–60 (50–150)	yellow, floating plant
water chestnut	*Trapa natans*	July–August, sun/half-shade	12–24 (30–60)	white, floating plant, some varieties have edible fruit
least yellow pondlily	*Nuphar pumila*	July–August, sun	10–20 (25–50)	yellow, floating plant
water fringe	*Nymphoides peltata*	July–August, sun/half-shade	10–20 (25–50)	yellow, floating plant, similar to waterlily, leaves much smaller, vigorous
amphibious bistort	*Polygonum amphibium*	July–August, sun/half-shade	4–16 (10–40)	red, floating plant, propagates vigorously by means of runners, regarded as a weed
duckweed	*Lemna minor*	sun/half-shade	0–40 (0–100)	floating plant, spreads like weeds
fairy moss	*Azolla caroliniana*	sun/half-shade	0–40 (0–100)	floating fern, forms a thick carpet but easily controlled

More plants for deep water or moderate depths

English name	botanical name	flowering period and position	depth of water in inches (cm)	flower colour, other remarks
mare's tail	*Hippuris vulgaris*	May–July, sun/half-shade	4–12 (10–30)	green, needle-like leaves, regarded as a weed
greater spearwort	*Ranunculus lingua* 'Grandiflora'	June–July, sun	4–8 (10–20)	yellow, grows tall and profusely
flowering rush	*Butomus umbellatus*	June–August, sun	4–8 (10–20)	pink to red, very pretty flowers
common arrowhead	*Sagittaria sagittifolia*	June–August, sun	4–8 (10–20)	white, decorative leaves and flowers
pickerel weed	*Pontederia cordata*	July–Sept., sun	4–8 (10–20)	blue, long-flowering, grows anywhere
wild rice	*Zizania latifolia*	sun/half-shade	16–20 (40–50)	height 5-6 ft (150–180 cm), robust, remains attractive into winter, annual

*Mare's tail (*Hippuris vulgaris*)*

*Pickerel weed (*Pontederia cordata)

*Flowering rush (*Butomus umbellatus)

More plants for deep water or moderate depths

English name	botanical name	flowering period and position	depth of water in inches (cm)	flower colour, other remarks
	Carex pseudocyperus	June–July, sun/half-shade	4-12 (10-30)	green, very pretty overhanging panicles, regarded as a weed
zebra rush	*Scirpus tabernaemontani* 'Zebrinus'	July–August, sun/half-shade	4-8 (10-20)	highly decorative, with green and white barred foliaged
bulrush	*Scirpus lacustris*	July–August, sun/half-shade	4-12 (10-30)	dark green, growns profusely in a favourable position
sweet flag	*Acorus calamus*	July–August, sun/half-shade	4-8 (10-20)	green, iris-like habit, an old strewing herb
foil plant	*Marsilea quadrifolia*	sun	4-8 (10-20)	water fern with clover-like leaves, not very hardy, usually grown in aquaria
willow moss	*Fontinalis antipyretica*	sun	8-12 (20-30)	likes running water

61

Plants for the marginal zone

The marginal zone contains many beautiful and adaptable plants. The flowers begin in spring with marsh marigold (*Caltha palustris*) and bog bean (*Menyanthes trifoliata*), leading on to yellow flag (*Iris pseuda-corus*) and flowering rush (*Butomus umbellatus*) during the summer. Flowering continues with water plantain (*Alisma plantago-aquatica*) until the last butterflies settle on the Joe Pye weed (*Eupatorium purpureum*) in the last days of autumn.

Such plants can't afford to be too sensitive. In the wild, too, the water level may sometimes fall dramatically, and they are scarcely harmed provided they don't dry out completely. They can also cope with high water levels. Creeping Jenny (*Lysi-machia nummularia*) survives particularly well, spreading quickly around the pond to mask all those ugly edges. In June it covers everything with a thick carpet of green, and produces masses of golden flowers. Creeping Jenny also grows well without any water, either in a pot or as a ground-cover plant in the garden.

In preformed ponds these plants find their home in the marginal zones. In lined ponds they prefer the broader, shallow banks.

Troughs, barrels and small ponds can be similarly planted with marginal vegetation. It's less important to develop an ecologically balanced plant community next to the house. You can even mix a few exotics with native plants to create a pleasant combination of colours and shapes.

A good choice is the common arrowhead (*Sagittaria sagitti-folia*) with its arrow-shaped leaves and long-lasting display of yellowish-white flowers. Pickerel weed (*Pontederia

cordata) from North America has lovely steel-blue flowers, but isn't very hardy. The bog bean (*Menyanthes trifoliata*) grows vigorously, producing pure-white, delicately fringed flowers in May. The water forget-me-not (*Myosotis palustris*) is covered with sky-blue flowers from May right through to October. Its decorative shoots go well not only with the grass-like leaves of the reedmace, but also with the round, flat leaves of the water-lily and the fleshier leaves of the bistort (*Polygonum bistorta*).

Irises produce some of the most beautiful blooms of all, including the violet-blue flowers of the North American flag (*Iris versicolor*), and those of the blue water iris (*Iris laevigata*) with their pink, blue and white colouring. The flowers of the clematis-flowered iris (*Iris kaempferi*) have almost circular petals that are arranged hori-zontally. This bog plant is unusual in requiring a wet position in the summer and a dry one in the winter. This means that you need to create a special planting area for it, or else move it around in a special container.

Blue water iris (Iris laevigata)

The most important marginal plants (in order of flowering)

English name	botanical name	flowering period and position	depth of water in inches (cm)	growth height in inches (cm)	flower colour, other remarks
white skunk cabbage	*Lysichiton camtschatcense*	March–April sun/half-shade	0	12–16 (30–40)	white
marsh marigold	*Caltha palustris*	April–May, sun/half-shade	0–4 (0–10)	8–12 (20–30)	yellow, hardy, vigorous
bog bean	*Menyanthes trifoliata*	April–May, sun/half-shade	2–4 (5–10)	8–12 (20–30)	white
cotton grass	*Eriophorum angustifolium*	April–July, sun/half-shade	0–4 (0–10)	12–16 (30–40)	white, fast-spreading, must have acid conditions
yellow flag	*Iris pseudacorus*	May–June, sun/half-shade	2–8 (5–20)	12–40 (30–100)	yellow, vigorous, flowers profusely
bistort	*Polygonum bistorta*	May–July, sun/half-shade	0–12 (0–30)	24–32 (60–80)	pink, fast-spreading
blue water iris	*Iris laevigata*	June–July, sun/half-shade	0–6 (0–15)	24–32 (60–80)	blue, tolerates standing water all year round, red, pink and white varieties
bur-reed	*Sparganium erectum*	June–Sept., sun	2–8 (5–20)	12–25 (30–60)	whitish-green
creeping Jenny	*Lysimachia nummularia*	June–Sept., sun/half-shade	+4–4 (+10–10)	2 (5)	yellow, ground-cover plant, hides ugly edges
yellow musk	*Minulus luteus*	June–Sept., sun	0–6 (0–15)	8–10 (20–25)	yellow, spreads quickly by seeding
water forget-me-not	*Myosotis palustris*	June–Oct., sun	+4–4 (+10–10)	12–16 (30–40)	sky-blue, flowers profusely, spreads its own seeds
purple loosestrife	*Lythrum salicaria*	July–Sept., sun/half-shade	+4–4 (+10–10)	28–40 (70–100)	carmine red, attracts butterflies
water plantain	*Alisma plantago-aquatica*	July–Sept., sun/half-shade	+2–8 (+5–20)	12–28 (30–70)	white/pinkish, flowers like baby's breath (*Gypsophila*)
common reedmace	*Typha latifolia*	Sept.–Nov., sun	4–12 (10–30)	60–72 (150–180)	dark brown, proliferates, long-lasting flowers

More marginal plants (in order of flowering)

English name	botanical name	flowering period and position	depth of water in inches (cm)	growth height in inches (cm)	flower colour, other remarks
golden club	*Orontium aquaticum*	May–June, sun	0–8 (0–20)	12–16 (30–40)	white–yellow, striking appearance
marsh helleborine	*Epipactis palustris*	May–June, sun/half-shade	+4–0 (+10–0)	12 (30)	greenish-white, orchid for unfertilised position, rare threatened plant
copper musk	*Mimulus cupreus*	May–July, sun/half-shade	0–4 (0–10)	8 (20)	coppery red, pretty, flowers profusely
various orchids	*Dactylorhiza* species	May–July, sun/half-shade	+4–0 (+10–0)	12–16 (30–40)	speckled pink, red, protected species, available under cultivation
marsh spurge	*Euphorbia palustris*	May–July, sun/half-shade	+4–2 (+10–5)	20–32 (50–80)	green–yellow, spreads easily in a favourable position
brooklime	*Veronica beccabunga*	May–August, sun	4–6 (10–15)	9–15 (23–38)	blue, goes well with irises
North American flag	*Iris versicolor*	June–July, sun	2–4 (5–10)	24–28 (60–70)	violet, won't tolerate deep water
cardinal flower	*Lobelia cardinalis*	June–Sept., sun/half-shade	0–4 (0–10)	24–32 (60–80)	bright red, striking appearance, long-flowering

Purple loosestrife (Lythrum) and meadowsweet (Filipendula)

Yellow musk (Mimulus)

*Bog bean (*Menyanthes trifoliata) *Marsh marigold (*Caltha palustris)

English name	botanical name	flowering period and position	depth of water in inches (cm)	growth height in inches (cm)	flower colour, other remarks
variegated reed	*Phragmites australis* 'Variegatus'	July, sun/half-shade	0–4 (0–10)	48–60 (120–150)	brownish-red, striking appearance, leaves with cream stripes
lizard's tail	*Saururus cernuus*	July–August, sun/half-shade	0–4 (0–10)	24–48 (60–120)	yellowish-white, pendulous flowers, red autumn foliage
soft rush	*Juncus ensifolius*	July–August, sun/half-shade	0–6 (0–15)	20–24 (50–60)	dark brown, regarded as a weed
least bur-reed	*Sparganium minimum*	July–Sept., sun	2–6 (5–15)	8–12 (20–30)	whitish-green, chestnut-like flowers, regarded as a weed
marsh gentian	*Gentiana pneumonanthe*	July–Sept., sun	+4–0 (+10–0)	12–16 (30–40)	deep blue, peatland plant
Joe Pye weed	*Eupatorium purpureum*	July–Oct., sun	+4–0 (+10–0)	60–80 (150–200)	purplish-red, good for cut flowers
water musk	*Mimulus ringens*	Sept.–Oct., sun	+12–0 (+30–0)	16–24 (40–60)	blue, very pretty
narrow-leaved reedmace	*Typha angustifolia*	Sept.–Nov., sun	4–8 (10–20)	40–52 (100–130)	dark brown, narrow, long-flowering
dwarf reedmace	*Typha minima*	Sept.–Nov., sun/half-shade	4–8 (10–20)	40–48 (100–120)	dark brown, short cob-like appearance

Plants around the pond

The pond isn't the only element of a water garden. It needs to be planted in a way that matches the surrounding garden, including trees and shrubs, walls and stones, paths and wooden palisades, not to mention any pergolas or other design features. But the most important elements are the herbaceous borders right next to the pond. It's best to choose a loose, natural-looking arrangement for this area, alternating tall grasses, irises and bamboos with various low-growing herbaceous plants and shrubs.

It goes almost without saying that you should aim for an assortment of plants that will extend the flowering season as much as possible. This is why the plants in the tables above and below have been ordered according to the time when they come into flower.

Your display will also look much more attractive if you plant whole groups of plants, each of the same variety or species, rather than mixing up plants of different species. The tables that follow include mainly those plants that are wilder in character, and those that are most suitable for planting near a pond because of their natural habitat.

There are many more plants you could choose from — you only need to look around you! There are hosts of different summer flowers you could use, not to mention the various flowering shrubs such as azaleas (with flowers in soft or striking colours), rhododendrons and brooms. All these plants need a good soil with plenty of water and humus. So don't stint on the compost, tree bark, peat and the other elements that go to make up a good planting medium.

Keep the weeds down in your herbaceous borders with plenty of mulching — i.e. covering the soil with well-rotted shreds of wood, bark and sawdust.

*Himalayan cowslip (*Primula florindae)

Lungwort (Pulmonaria angustifolia)

Elephant's ears (Bergenia cordifolia)

The most important plants around the pond (in order of flowering)

English name	botanical name	flowering period and position	depth of water in inches (cm)	flower colour, other remarks
elephant's ears	*Bergenia cordifolia*	March–April, sun/half-shade	8-12 (20-30)	pink, very robust, often flowers again in autumn
	Primula rosea	March–April, sun/half-shade	2-4 (5-10)	pink, needs boggy conditions and full sun
lungwort	*Pulmonaria agustifolia*	March–April, sun/half-shade	6-12 (15-30)	blue, pretty, speckled leaves, plant for bees
drumstick primula	*Primula denticulata*	March–April, half-shade	4-8 (10-20)	lilac, white, bluish, spherical flowers, can stand dryish conditions
leopard's bane	*Doronicum caucasicum*	April–May, sun/half-shade	20-24 (50-60)	yellow, flowers profusely, divide every 3 or 4 years
cowslip	*Primula veris*	April–May, sun/half shade	6-10 (15-25)	yellow, needs full sun
globe flower	*Trollius europaeus*	April–June, sun/half-shade	20-32 (50-80)	yellow, very good for cut flowers
	Brunnera macrophylla	April–June, Sun/half-shade	12-24 (30-60)	blue, long-flowering
Siberian iris	*Iris sibirica*	May–June, sun/half-shade	24-32 (60-80)	deep blue, forms large clumps of flowers in damp locations

More plants around the pond (in order of flowering)

English name	botanical name	flowering period and position	depth of water in inches (cm)	flower colour, other remarks
bugle	*Ajuga reptans*	May–July, sun/half-shade	6–8 (15–20)	light blue, creeping habit, ground-cover plant
Jacob's ladder	*Polemonium caeruleum*	May–Sept., sun/half-shade	20–28 (50–70)	blue/white, flowers profusely, seeds itself
meadow cranesbill	*Geranium pratense*	June–July, sun/half-shade	20–24 (50–60)	light blue
goatsbeard	*Aruncus sylvester*	June–July, sun/half-shade	32–48 (80–120)	white, also tolerates extreme shade
clematis-flowered iris	*Iris kaempferi*	June–July, sun	27–28 (67–70)	pink, blue, looks magnificent, grow in wet soil
spiderwort	*Tradescantia virginiana*	June–August, sun/half-shade	16–24 (40–60)	blue/white, grows profusely
daylily	*Hemerocallis* varieties	June–August, sun/half-shade	28–32 (70–80)	yellow, brown, russet, note new varieties and colours, older varieties wilder in character
lady's mantle	*Alchemilla mollis*	June–August, sun/half-shade	12–16 (30–40)	greenish-yellow, veil-like flowers, foliage good for vases
Himalayan cowslip	*Primula florindae*	June–August sun/half-shade	16–20 (40–50)	yellow, fragrant, long-flowering
false goatsbeard	*Astilbe* species and varieties	July–August, sun/half-shade	20–32 (50–80)	white, pink, red, ideal for damp, half-shaded locations

*Siberian iris (*Iris sibirica*)*

*Wild orchid (*Dactylorhiza*)*

*Meadow cranesbill (*Geranium pratense*)*

*Turtle-head (*Chelone obliqua*)*

*False goatsbeard (*Astilbe*)*

More plants around the pond (in order of flowering)

English name	botanical name	flowering period and position	depth of water in inches (cm)	flower colour, other remarks
plantian lily	*Hosta* species and varieties	July–August, sun/half-shade	12–24 (30–60)	soft blue or white, pretty-coloured leaves (blue-green or yellow-striped)
	Ligularia przewalskii	July–August, sun/half-shade	35–56 (90–140)	yellow, flowers profusely
Kansas feather	*Liatris spicata*	July–August, sun/half-shade	24–32 (60–80)	lilac, flowers from top to bottom, attracts butterflies
red-hot poker	*Kniphofia uvaria*	July–August, sun/half-shade	24–32 (60–80)	red-yellow
	Inula magnifica	July–Sept., sun/half-shade	60–100 (150–250)	yellow, impressive appearance, much-visited by bees
yellow loosestrife	*Lysimachia punctata*	July–Sept., sun/half-shade	24–40 (60–100)	yellow, indestructible, proliferates, long-flowering
purple coneflower	*Echinacea purpurea*	August–Sept., sun/half-shade	24–40 (60–100)	purplish-pink, large, expressive flowers, attracts butterflies
marsh gladiolus	*Gladiolus palustris*	August–Oct., sun	24–28 (60–70)	pink speckled, unusual appearance, hardy, plant in damp soil
Japanese anemone	*Anemone japonica*	August–Oct., sun/half-shade	24–40 (60–100)	white/pink, pastel shades, elegant flowers into late autumn
turtle-head	*Chelone obliqua*	August–Oct., sun/half-shade	24–28 (60–70)	pink, indestructible, long-flowering
willow-leaved sunflower	*Helianthus salicifolius*	Sept.–Oct., sun/half-shade	72–100 (180–250)	yellow, interesting, graceful habit, no flowers
snakeroot	*Cimicifuga racemosa*	Sept.–Nov., sun/half-shade	24–56 (60–140)	white, brings a late splash of colour into the garden

PLANTS FOR THE POND

Some attractive ferns

English name	botanical name	position	growth height in inches (cm)	other remarks
American maidenhair fern	*Adiantum pedatum*	half-shade	8-16 (20-40)	—
hard fern	*Blechnum spicant*	half-shade	8-12 (20-30)	evergreen
royal fern	*Osmunda regalis*	half-shade	32-48 (80-120)	—
hart's tongue fern	*Phyllitis scolopendrium*	half-shade	12-16 (30-40)	evergreen

Royal fern (Osmunda regalis)

American maidenhair fern (Adiantum pedatum)

*Bamboo (*Sinarundinaria murielae*)*

*Pampas grass (*Cortaderia selloana*)*

Some attractive grasses

English name	botanical name	flowering period and position	growth height in inches (cm)	other remarks
blue oat	*Avena candida*	June–July, sun	24–32 (60–80)	white, narrow blue-green leaves
	Stipa barbata	June–August, sun	24–32 (60–80)	white, attractive in winter too
pampas grass	*Cortaderia selloana*	August–Oct., sun	60–80 (150–200)	white/reddish, in winter can't tolerate stagnant wetness
Chinese fountain grass	*Pennisetum compressum*	August–Oct., sun	20–32 (50–80)	reddish-green, long, pendant flowers
	Miscanthus sinensis	sun	72–120 (180–300)	very impressive appearance

How to grow tropical and subtropical plants

There is a wide choice of native water plants, including a number of very beautiful species that can survive the winter without any difficulty. Just look at a flooded area of woodland — those pink clouds of flowering water violets (*Hottonia palustris*), together with arrowhead (*Sagittaria*) — and wild arum, royal fern and Solomon's seal (*Polygonatum*) and you will find little to distinguish our native flora from that to be found in tropical streams.

However, there's also something to be said for strange and exotic plants — and not only because of their beautiful colours and shapes. They also present a challenge to any gardener who wants to grow water hyacinths, lotus flowers, rice and arum lilies in our climate. The main problem is overwintering. You need a space that is well-lit and frost-free, but is also cooler than normal room temperature so the plants can become dormant: 50–60°F (10–15°C) is just about ideal. A conservatory or warm greenhouse often provides just the right conditions.

The plants described below can also be planted in indoor containers — an idea that's catching on fast. You could also add a number of popular pot plants such as a peace lily

(*Spathiphyllum wallisii*) from a garden centre, or one or two of the various bromeliads.

The **fairy moss** (*Azolla caroliniana*) is a pretty floating fern with small emerald-green leaves that turn red-brown in autumn. It grows vigorously, and in mild

winters it can be left in the open throughout.

Indian shot (*Canna indica*) is normally cultivated in dry conditions, where it grows and flowers profusely as a bedding plant. However, it originally came from marshy areas and grows well as a marginal plant. This Indian species bears red or yellow flowers, and grows to a height of 65 inches (160 cm). Its close relative *Canna flaccida* comes from the southern United

States; it has sulphur-yellow flowers and grows as high as 68 inches (170 cm). If possible, the fleshy rhizomes should be overwintered in a cellar until the end of February, and then planted out in soil with plenty of humus.

Umbrella grass (*Cyperus alternifolius*) is well known as a houseplant. Not so well known is the fact that it comes from marshy regions, and that its leaves react to dry conditions by yellowing at the tips. It can easily be propagated by placing a leaf upside-down in water. In a large tub it will grow quickly to form an attractive clump measuring 16-24 inches (40-60 cm) in height. In summer this plant will grow better in a garden pond: simply place the container in the water, and fetch it out again to bring it indoors for the winter. This plant will grow in water depths of 0-12 inches (0-30 cm).

Papyrus (*Cyperus papyrus*) is a closely related plant that grows vigorously in boggy conditions. Papyrus thickets on the banks of African rivers can easily grow as high as 10 ft (3 m). In this country the plant reaches 5 ft-6 ft 6 in (150-200 cm) at the most. The ancient Egyptians used to take the pith from the long, triangular leaves and stick several layers together to create papyrus, an early fore-runner of paper. This imposing pot plant lends a tropical flavour to any water garden. Papyrus grows best at depths of 16-20 inches (40-50 cm). Overwinter it in a conservatory at temperatures of 60-65°F (15-18°C), giving it as much light as possible.

The **water hyacinth** (*Eichhornia crassipes*) is a lovely floating plant with blue flowers and swollen leaf stems. Although it's commonly available when in bloom, it doesn't propagate or flower very readily in our climate. It needs large amounts of sun and a warm, sheltered position to flower and grow vigorously. The rivers of its native Central and South America provide such ideal conditions that it proliferates there out of all control, creating a barrier to shipping. The beard-shaped roots filter and clean the

The Indian lotus flower is one of the most remarkable water plants. The stemmed fruits are sometimes used in flower arrangements.

73

water. The more nutrients they absorb, the more flowers they produce between June and September. The leathery leaves will also stifle the growth of unwanted algae by depriving them of light. You should overwinter this plant in shallow bowls at temperatures of 45-50°F (8-10°C), giving it plenty of light.

The **water poppy** (*Hydrocleys commersonii*) has 3-inch (8-cm) long floating leaves that resemble those of the waterlily. The flowers are yellow and cup-shaped, measuring some 2 inches (5 cm) in diameter and rising up above the surface of the water. Many new flowers appear every day from June right through to October. The water poppy needs full sunlight. You should overwinter it in bowls at a temperature of 50-55°F (10-12°C). The water poppy can also be grown as a houseplant.

The lovely **cardinal flower** (*Lobelia cardinalis*) with its fiery-red blooms is a good plant for vases or pond margins. It also flourishes in flower beds, although it prefers the wetter environment next to a pond. Unfortunately this plant isn't hardy, so it should be over-wintered in a cool, well-lit room. The cardinal flower grows to a height of 24-32 inches (60-80 cm) and produces flowers from June to September.

Parrot's feather (*Myriophyllum proserpinacoidae*) has dense, bright-green, needle-like leaves that grow both above and below the water surface, and eventually cover the pond. It's a popular aquarium plant with insignificant flowers, and can be overwintered in a living room. The plant's English name reflects the structure of the leaves, which are long and finely divided, just like the feathers of a parrot.

Indian shot thrives in both wet and dry conditions, and is noted for its striking flowers.

Papyrus grows to 10 ft (3 m) in the African marshes.

Lotus flowers (*Nelumbo*) are the subject of many legends, and have almost come to symbolise the tropics. The best-known species is the Indian lotus (*Nelumbo nucifera*), which is native to southern Asia but has also spread into southern Europe. The Indian lotus is a difficult and demanding plant to grow in our climate. It requires so much warmth that extra heating is often needed, even in the summer. This plant bears round, blue-green leaves on long stems. Its beautiful pink flowers look similar to water-lilies, but grow on even taller stems. The fruits, which are shaped rather like the rose of a watering can, are popular in dried flower arrangements.

Lotus flowers can be over-wintered as rhizomes. The thin, banana-shaped rhizomes are fragile and must be handled with great care. They will not survive without the tips of the shoots. Lotus flowers need to be planted beneath shallow water in a 12-16-inch (30–40-cm) layer of well-fertilised, nutritious soil. They need full sunlight, and must be sheltered from the wind (preferably by a wall). They are easy to transport if you put them in a deep basket made of plastic. Lotus flowers may be difficult to grow, but their beauty more than repays the effort.

Daubeny's waterlily (*Nymphaea* × *daubenyana*) is an interesting hybrid waterlily whose unusual blue flowers make up for the fact that it isn't hardy. There are a number of brightly coloured varieties. The large flowers measure as much as 4-6 inches (10-15 cm) across, and grow about a hand's breadth above the surface of the water. They also give off a beautiful scent. This is just one of many lovely tropical water-lilies, some of which flower only at night. Fortunately, however, the majority flower in the daytime.

Tropical waterlilies should be planted in about 12 inches (30 cm) of soil beneath shallow or moderately deep water — about 20-28 inches (50-70 cm). The required temperatures — 77°F (25°C) in summer and 68°F (20°C) in winter — mean that you'll want some additional heating. These plants also need plenty of light, so a conservatory is probably the best location for growing them in.

Rice (*Oryza sativa*) is well known as a food plant. It flourishes in the paddies and terraces of southeastern Asia, where it enjoys a much warmer climate than here.

This annual grass can be grown from seed by planting unpeeled grains in a plant pot in March. The seedlings will start to sprout after three weeks, and you should repot them in larger pots of nutritious soil containing plenty of loam but no peat. From now on they need lots of moisture. The best position is in shallow water with plenty of light and warmth (68-86°F/ 20-30°C). The plants will grow to between 20 inches (50 cm) and 5 ft (150 cm) depending on the variety. By autumn they will have formed gracefully nodding panicles that should, with luck, be self-pollinating.

If possible you should always choose an early variety. Experience suggests that the best varieties for our somewhat hostile climate are Philippine mountain rice and the Italian varieties. Never confuse true rice with wild rice (*Zizania*), a completely different plant that will survive even the coldest of our winters.

The **arum lily** (*Zantedeschia aethiopica*) was a popular and much-prized greenhouse plant in Victorian times, when it was even used for funeral wreaths. Arum lilies have made a comeback in recent years, and are available from the majority of garden centres, either as dormant rootstocks or as fully grown plants in flower.

In summer they will grow best if you plant them in shallow water. They start to flower in

The arum lily (Zantedeschia aethiopica) was a popular green-house plant in Victorian times. The rootstocks will produce a glorious display every year.

Water poppies flower profusely in a sunny position.

Rice is a highly decorative grass. In hot summers the nodding flowers will develop to form ripe grains.

June and carry on into the autumn, when you should stop watering them in order to let them die back naturally. After the dormant period is over, you should replant the rootstocks in nutritious soil with plenty of humus, and let them sprout until May. Apart from the usual white forms of arum lily, there are other varieties with yellow or pink flowers.

Fish for the pond

Ornamental fish can make a very colourful and interesting addition to your pond, but you should be aware of the problems they bring with them. They need a protein-rich diet in order to thrive — and what could be richer in protein than the eggs and larvae of the other animals that live in the pond, not to mention tadpoles and immature fish. Additional feeding can also create problems: if you give them too much, the left-overs will increase the nutrient level in the water. It's difficult to regain the ecological balance, and in the mean time a sudden rise in water temperature could be enough to kill the whole pond.

There are fewer problems in a larger pond that has plenty of nooks and crannies and underwater vegetation. Some of the tiny creatures can hide here to escape their predators, and you won't need to give your fish any extra food, either.

How many fish can a garden pond support? The answer is governed by many different factors, and it's impossible to generalise. The size and social behaviour of the different fish species varies enormously, as does their speed of growth and the amount of space they need. An aquarium can accommodate a large number of fish in a small space, but even here there are limits: a single 2-inch (5-cm)

long fish needs at one square foot (900 cm²) of water surface in order to live.

What species should you choose? One factor to bear in mind here is the natural temperament of the fish. Goldfish and

orfes, for example, get used to people so quickly that after a while you can persuade them to feed out of your hand. Some fish do nothing but swim around, which can become boring after a while. In this respect the playful orfes have more to offer than the sluggish koi carp. However, looks can be important, too, and brightly coloured fish

are more clearly visible than dark-coloured ones.

When you introduce fish into your pond, make sure to plant plenty of underwater vegetation beforehand. Although many fish nibble at it, they are rarely (if ever) poisoned by it. On the contrary, they benefit from the extra oxygen it provides, and in a sunny pond this can be vital to survival. They lay their eggs among the leaves. Immature and aging fish can hide there, often from their own kind — for hungry parents have no compunction about eating their own offspring.

Carry newly bought fish in a plastic bag, and place this unopened in the pond for no more than twenty minutes so the fish can get used to the new water temperature. To avoid importing any fish diseases, keep your new arrivals in a separate basin for one or two weeks. Water quality is very important. A pH value of 6-7 is preferable (i.e. just on the acid side of neutral). The water can easily become polluted, so it's advisable to install a filter from the start.

Goldfish come in many different colours and shapes. They're among the hardiest pond fish, and get used to people very easily.

Feeding the fish

Often there's not enough water surface available for fish, or enough plants, larvae, frog-spawn or algae for them to feed on. However, their appetite is strongly influenced by the water temperature. They become dormant under 50°F (10°C), and their appetite is only aroused when the temperature rises above this, so you may need to feed them a little more from April to the end of October.

The fish food you can buy over the counter comes in the form of flakes, and contains a good mixture of carbohydrates, proteins, fats, minerals, vitamins and trace elements. The flakes stay at the surface for 10-15 minutes before sinking to the bottom. Any food that still hasn't been eaten at this stage is surplus to requirements, so at the next feeding you should reduce the amount accordingly. Otherwise the water will gain too many nutrients, which will encourage the growth of algae. Left-overs from meals are not suitable as fish food.

You can teach fish to respond to repeated sounds such as taps or clicks that tell them it's feeding time. They can become so trusting that they'll even feed out of your hand.

Fish for an ornamental pond

With fish and animals, as with plants, there's one golden rule you should follow: always buy from a bona fide supplier. In any case, the capture of many wild animals is forbidden (or at very least regulated) by law — not to mention the risk of bringing unwanted diseases into your pond.

A garden pond should be a place of peace and quiet, so there's no sense in buying predators such as perch, or species like sticklebacks that multiply very quickly. Trout, barbel and gudgeon need a continuous supply of fresh, running water, so they certainly aren't suitable for a pond with standing water.

Even so, this still leaves an extremely wide choice of species that *are* suitable for garden ponds.

The **bitterling** (*Rhodeus sericeus*) is a small relative of the carp that is native to Europe. It's just 2-4 inches (6-9 cm) long, and is remarkable for its symbiotic relationship with the swan mussel. At spawning time the female bitterling lays a few eggs in the breathing hole of each mussel. The male follows and sprays its milt over the same places. The mussel's breathing ensures that the eggs are fertilised and get plenty of oxygen during the next three to four weeks. When the young bitterling come to leave their adopted parent, they are fully equipped to swim.

Minnows (*Phoxinus phoxinus*) easily become accustomed to being with people, and can also be trained. They're only small, measuring just 2-4 inches (5-10 cm), and are extremely gregarious. The males develop a striking colour pattern during the breeding season.

Goldfish (*Carassius auratus*) also become accustomed to people very easily. They're among the most popular of pond fish, partly because of their glorious red or yellow colouring, which comes in many variations. They're also extremely easy to look after, and can readily survive the winter in a garden pond. They often don't develop their distinctive colouring until their second year, as the water temperature rises. Immature goldfish are similar to their wild ancestor, the silver carp from Asia. Among the best-known ornamental forms of goldfish are the veiltail and the scaleless shubunkin from Japan.

The **golden and silver orfe** (*Leuciscus idus*) are both elegant and gregarious. They are silver-coloured in the wild; the golden form is an ornamental variant. They're among the liveliest of fish, swarming along

Bitterlings lay their eggs in the breathing holes of mussels.

Minnows are small, lively and very gregarious.

Catfish and ornamental koi carp from Japan — both are well suited to our climate

The **roach** (*Rutilus rutilus*) is a gregarious fish that's very suitable for ornamental ponds because it doesn't feed on water plants. There is also a gold-coloured ornamental form.

The **tench** (*Tinca tinca*) is similar to the carp, but smaller. It likes to hide near the bed of the pond, where it eagerly snaps up any fish food that sinks to the bottom. There are also white and gold-coloured ornamental forms.

the surface and leaping up to catch gnats. They soon become tame if you feed them, and grow quickly to a maximum length of 20 inches (50 cm).

The **crucian carp** (*Carassius carassius*) is closely related to the goldfish and similarly un-demanding. It's fond of bottom-feeding, browsing mainly on soft plant material. It's also suited to small ponds. It is shiny and golden yellow in colour.

In its original, dark-grey form the **common carp** (*Cyprinus carpio*) is a popular food fish in Central Europe. It needs a large pond and specialised food. The Japanese ornamental forms, known as **koi carp**, are much prized for their striking colours. They can cope with shallow

pools, but always need plenty of fresh water. This, together with their large size (16–20 in/40–50 cm), means that only a large pond is suitable. Both common and koi carp feed on plant remains and specialised food.

Roach are well suited to ornamental ponds.

Garden and pond animals

You can buy fish for your pond, but the wild animals described below can't be bought at any price. Their arrival in a new pond is a cause for celebration because it shows that the pond has achieved a natural balance, and that it has become an environment that's attractive to new animals.

A new pond is quickly noticed from the air, attracting insects such as beetles, dragonflies and gnats, which rarely become a problem in a well-balanced environment. However, amphibians such as frogs, toads and newts are somewhat fussier. Their requirements include the following:

- plenty of peace and quiet away from possible disturbance by cats and dogs, which love to hunt them;
- an open, sunny area for them to bask in;
- plenty of bushes, plants, stones or walls to provide cover;
- shallow water to spawn in;
- lots of food (especially insects) available without human assistance.

Their chief enemies are fish, which feed on their eggs and on the larvae of insects. Tadpoles are especially vulnerable. After spawning in late winter or early spring, the jelly-like eggs develop into tadpoles within the

space of about three weeks. After hatching, the tiny tadpoles go in search of food; gnat larvae are a special delicacy. They grow quickly, and within eight weeks they have become small but fully formed frogs.

The main species

The **edible frog** (*Rana esculenta*) is rare in Britain but common in France, where its hind legs are considered a great delicacy. It readily colonises new ponds, jumping and diving amid the waterlilies. This frog can become very tame, and is only a nuisance for a few nights

The edible frog isn't common, but is very much at home in garden ponds.

The hawker dragonfly (Aeshna cyanea) is a remarkably accomplished flier.

during the spawning season (April– May), when its mating calls can be very loud. The colouring varies, but is generally muddy green with lighter and darker stripes on the back.

The edible frog feeds mainly on mosquito larvae and insects on the wing, which it catches with its long tongue. You can tempt it out of the pond by offering it live worms, but it normally prefers to hide among the water plants or under bushes around the pond.

The **hawker dragonfly**

(Aeshna cyanea) is beautifully equipped for flying, achieving speeds of up to 30 mph (50 km/h); it can even fly backwards. Dragonflies are predators, but are never harmful to humans despite their sometimes threatening appearance.

An adult dragonfly lives no longer than one summer. It lays its eggs on the leaves of water plants, and especially under waterlily leaves. As soon as the larva hatches, it starts to feed voraciously on mosquito larvae, snails' eggs, fish spawn and even tadpoles. The larval period varies from one to five years depending on the species. The final emergence of the dragonfly on a stem or leaf is a fascinating process to watch, and can often be seen on a garden pond.

The hawker dragonfly is greenish in colour and grows to about 3 inches (7–8 cm) in length. It is a relatively common species. But there are about 60 others, some of which are just as common around ponds.

The **smooth newt** (*Triturus vulgaris*) is just one of three

native species of newt. Newts and salamanders are amphibians, like frogs and toads, but are different in retaining their tails after the tadpole stage.

Smooth newts are common in ponds, especially in the east of Britain. They are difficult to spot because they dive underwater at the slightest sign of danger. They are also well camouflaged against the pond bed. If you wait patiently, however, you may see them come up for air. You may even get a glimpse of their colourfully patterned bellies, which are particularly striking in spawning males. Newts feed at night on worms, water fleas and various small water insects.

Newts spawn at night in the early spring, laying their eggs individually in the folds of underwater leaves. In June they leave the water and find cool places to hide during the day — under leaves or moss, for example. But they normally return to the same place to spawn. This means that if you catch newts and let them loose in your pond, you won't be able to keep them for very long. In winter they hibernate, usually under a pile of stones.

The two other native newt species have very similar habits and lifestyles to the smooth newt. But they are different in appearance and in distribution. Further details about both these species are given overleaf.

A smooth newt (Triturus vulgaris)

The common frog is perhaps the best-loved of all our garden animals

The **palmate newt** (*Triturus helveticus*) is smaller than the smooth newt but very similar in appearance. The tail, however, is differently shaped, and the feet become webbed during the spawning season. Although found less frequently in the east of Britain, it is commoner than the smooth newt in the west.

The **crested newt** (*Triturus cristatus*) is much less common than the smooth newt, but is noticeably larger, and the skin is warty. The male is particularly distinctive during the spawning season, when it develops an impressive crest along its back. If you find a crested newt in your pond, do nothing to discourage it: in recent years it has become an endangered species.

The **common frog** (*Rana temporaria*) is among the best-loved and most familiar of all garden animals. Although smaller and less attractive than the edible frog, it is very much more common, and readily colonises ponds if the conditions are right. It is most frequently seen here during the spawning season (February–March). After that it prefers damp meadows and woodlands, where it hides among the grass and leaves. The common frog has a similar life cycle to that of its larger relative, the edible frog, but is easier to keep in a terrarium.

The **marsh frog** (*Rana ridibunda*), like the edible frog, is rare in this country, but is frequently seen in those areas where it does occur. It's very similar in colour to the common frog and follows much the same lifestyle, but is larger than both the other frogs.

The **common toad** (*Bufo bufo*) is remarkable for its homing instinct, often travelling more than 2 miles (3 km) in order to spawn in the pond where it grew up. (Attempts are now being made to protect this animal in places where a spawning pond lies close to a busy road.) When the toad eventually arrives at its pond, it lays as many as 5,000–6,000 eggs in long strings.

Toads are nocturnal animals. They perform a very useful role in gardens by feeding on snails, slugs, caterpillars and worms. Unfortunately they are often persecuted because of their rather unappealing appearance. Admittedly their earth-brown skin covered in warts and glands doesn't make them the most attractive of creatures. If cornered, they react by excreting a milky fluid from these glands. The acrid fluid is irritating to the skin, so you should only handle a toad with gloves on, and wash your hands thoroughly afterwards.

The common toad performs a useful role in killing off garden pests. It travels many miles back to its birthplace to spawn.

The **natterjack toad** (*Bufo calamita*) is similar to its much commoner relative. However, the back legs are shorter, which means that it runs instead of hopping. In some places it is actually known as the running toad. Although less inclined than the common toad to return to the same pond for spawning, it is if anything even more migratory. There is also evidence that its dwindling population may be due to migration across busy roads.

The **grass snake** (*Natrix natrix*) commonly visits ponds, where it feeds on frogs, toads and fish. It is longer and more slender than the poisonous adder, but is completely harmless. If you want to persuade a grass snake to stay around your pond, try feeding it with strips of raw meat until it gets used to being there.

Grass snakes are completely harmless.

The **swan mussel** (*Anodonta cygnea*) is common in garden ponds, and measures some 4-5 inches (10-12 cm) in length. It is a very useful animal to have in your pond: it ploughs through the mud filtering out the chalk to build up its shell, which improves the quality of the water. It also lives in a symbiotic relationship with the bitterling, providing a place for the fish's eggs to hatch. It feeds on tiny organisms and algae in the pond.

The great pond snail is extremely voracious.

The **great pond snail** (*Limnea stagnalis*) grows to a length of some 2-3 inches (6 cm), and can easily be recognised by its pointed spiral shell. It is extremely voracious, and also breeds very quickly if there are no fish in the pond. It isn't invariably a pest; for instance, it can be useful in getting rid of algae or rotting plant material. In general, though, it's a threat to plants, and should not be allowed to stay in any newly planted pond. You should check any plants that you introduce for eggs, and for the snails themselves. In fact, most pond snails should really be regarded as pests.

The **great ramshorn snail** (*Planorbius corneus*) looks very different: its shell is flatter, and shaped like a tiny French horn. Ramshorns are the only snails that can actually be recommended for a pond. They perform a useful function in removing algae, and search the pond bed for food, but rarely attack plants higher up in the pond.

Damselflies (*Coenagrion* species) are a small relative of the dragonfly. The glossy blue males and emerald-green females can be seen over the pond from spring onwards. The larvae are a dull brown colour.

The great diving beetle may be attractive to look at, but it's a vicious predator.

The **great diving beetle** (*Dytiscus marginalis*) is over an inch (3 cm) long and a lovely chocolate-brown colour. This handsome insect seems to appear as if from nowhere. Unfortunately it's a pest, and should be removed immediately with a butterfly net. Both the larvae and the mature insects prey on all kinds of pond life, and will even attack larger fish. Because this beetle is carnivorous, it can only be tolerated in a pond that's intended purely for plants.

Acilius sulcatus belongs to the same family as the great diving beetle. This brown insect also moves into the pond from elsewhere, and can be recognised by the grooves in the female's wing carapaces; those of the male beetle are smooth. Although equally predatory, it's less dangerous than its larger relative, living mostly on small insects. It is vulnerable to fish, so prefers to avoid them. It is an agile swimmer and diver.

Water fleas (*Daphnia* species) are perhaps one animal you can be guaranteed to find in your pond. These tiny 1-mm long crustaceans are often the first arrivals in a new pond. They multiply extremely fast, providing fish and other pond life with a ready supply of protein-rich food.

Mosquitoes, in particular the **common gnat** (*Culex pipiens*), are one of the more annoying creatures that live near water. They lay their eggs in water, especially in flooded woodlands, water butts and puddles. The larvae dive down into the depths at the slightest sign of danger. Mosquitoes are less of a problem in well-populated ponds because most of the larvae get eaten and fail to develop into adults.

The **pondskater** (*Gerris* species) is a remarkable insect. It literally walks on the water, taking advantage of the surface tension. It is commonest on ponds that have plants rather than animals in them.

 Ducks may prove an interesting addition to a large or medium-sized pond. The best choice are the semi-domestic breeds that can be kept in a fenced-off area. They can also make do with just a small area to swim in, and if you feed them intensively they can be fattened for eating.

What to do about the perennial problem of algae

Once a new pond has settled into a natural balance, there are generally no problems with algae. However, when algae do appear at this stage it's a sure sign that something is wrong. They only occur in large masses if there are too many nutrients dissolved in the water. In an emergency you could kill them off by chemical means, using a proprietary algicide that is harmless to both plants and animals. But the material left behind in the water will provide ample nutrients for further algal growth, so it's much better to tackle the root of the problem.

■ Newly laid ponds often contain free-floating green or brown algae, but these usually clear up quickly of their own accord.

■ Physically remove all yellowish-green filamentous algae using a rake or net. Repeat this process several times if necessary.

■ Don't give fish any more food than they absolutely need. Any food that sinks to the bottom will place a burden on the ecosystem.

■ Reduce water hardness by adding rainwater, or by hanging sacks of peat in the pond for a short time.

■ Don't add any fertiliser, and take measures to prevent nutrient-rich soil from being carried in by drainage from the surrounding land.

■ Add a selection of plants that combat algae by depriving them of light and nutrients — for example, waterlilies, starwort (*Callitriche*), hair grass (*Eleocharis*), hornwort (*Ceratophyllum*), water violet (*Hottonia*), milfoil (*Myriophyllu*m), water crowfoot (*Ranunculus aquatilis*), water soldier (*Stratiotes*), willow moss (*Fontinalis*), bladderwort (*Utricularia*), mare's tail (*Hippuris*) and brooklime (*Veronica beccabunga*).

Duckweed (*Lemna*) and Canadian pondweed (*Elodea*) both spread extremely fast. They may well make life very difficult for the algae, but they also bring problems of their own.

Filamentous algae will stifle everything in the pond, so you should remove them with a net. There are special algicides for use as a last resort.

Dealing with pests and diseases

Most garden ponds don't suffer from these problems, so the section that follows might seem superfluous. But water plants are occasionally attacked by pests and fungal diseases, and if this happens you'll need to know what to do about them.

The commonest fungal diseases

Crown rot (*Gleosporium nymphaearum*) is a disease that affects waterlilies. It occurs most commonly when you bring in plants or rhizomes that are already infected. Eventually it attacks the leaves, which gradually die; they become speckled with yellow and the edges hang limply.

The treatment is to replace the soil completely, and to destroy any plants that have been affected. If you wish, you can disinfect the pond bed by adding charcoal powder to it.

Leaf spot (*Phytomyces*) is yet another disease affecting waterlilies. Scabby dark-brown spots appear on the leaves and stems.

The best treatment is to spray the affected areas with a permitted fungicide. You'll need to take the planting basket out of the pond (or empty the pond) to reach all the affected places.

These holes are a sign of infestation by waterlily beetle larvae. All the affected leaves will have to be removed.

A variety of animal pests

Aphids often appear in large numbers. They can be found lurking on the underside of the leaves. These dark-brown insects nibble at the leaf tissue until large holes appear, and only the veins are left. You should cut off as many of the affected leaves as possible, and physically remove all the aphids. In most cases you just need to spray the affected areas with a strong jet of water, repeating the process if you don't manage to dislodge them the first time. Bear in mind that most insecticides are harmless to warm-blooded animals, but lethal to fish and other pond dwellers. This applies even to those insecticides (such as pyrethrum) that are derived from natural sources.

The **waterlily beetle** lays its eggs on the leaves. The larvae cut out whole pieces of leaf and roll themselves up in them. They then nibble away at them, working inwards from the outer edge. The only environmentally friendly solution is to remove the larvae bodily. In larger ponds these pests are eaten by ducks.

The **great pond snail** lives on plant tissue, and is particularly dangerous in a newly laid-out pond that doesn't yet have much in the way of vegetation. You should therefore check

Waterlily beetle larvae can inflict considerable damage, but only small plants are dangerously affected.

every leaf, and remove any eggs or snails that you find there. The great pond snail occasionally comes up to the surface for air, and you can remove it with the help of a net.

Voles are voracious rodents, and will happily gnaw through the pond liner so that the water leaks out, emptying the pond. One solution is to make an earthenware stopper to block up the hole and the area around it. However, it may be better to prevent the problem occurring in the first place by laying plastic-covered wire netting when you install the liner. If the liner is badly damaged, you may need to install a new liner, which will unfortunately in-volve clearing out the whole pond.

A working calendar for water gardeners

Spring (March–May)

As the winter draws to a close, the warmth and sunshine of early spring will tempt you out into the garden. Plants in and around the pond will be putting out their first green shoots, and soon frogs and newts will be busy spawning their young. March is one of the best times for an annual spring clean. Take the opportunity to remove all

Spring in a natural-looking garden. The pond shows hardly any signs of life, but the flowers and bulbs are already flourishing around its edges.

dead leaves and other plant material. Plants that are spreading too vigorously should be divided and replanted.

May is the time to make changes to the pond vegetation, adding new plants to replace those you've removed from areas where growth has become too dense. Empty the pond if absolutely necessary, but always leave plenty of water in the bottom to avoid the algae problems that can occur with new water. You could use soft rainwater to refill the pond (there's usually plenty of rain in late March and early April).

Summer (June–August)

Now everything is in full growth — including the algae. If there are too many filamentous algae, fish them out with a rake or a net. Check the waterlilies and other water plants for any pest infestation. Fish will also want regular feeding unless the pond is big enough to supply all their needs. If the pond starts to evaporate too quickly in the heat, add some more water to compensate. A drop of half an inch (10-15 mm) is quite normal on a hot day.

Keep a hole open in the winter ice so that air continues to circulate underneath.

Winter
(December–February)

In winter the pond remains largely dormant, but there are still processes going on that require an oxygen supply. This means it's important to encourage the exchange of gases to and from reed stems, bulrushes and other oxygenating plants in the pond. You should also keep a hole open in the winter ice. The best method is to use a small rubber ring that floats on the water and stops the water freezing inside it.

Otherwise you should leave nature to look after itself. Remove all water heaters and pumps, as they will disturb the natural temperature differences in the pond. The fish, for example, need the relatively warm layer (39°F/4°C) near the pond bed in order to survive. Don't hack at the ice if there are fish underneath: it could damage their swim bladders — and in any case they're extremely sensitive to noise. Any sound might arouse them from their winter sleep.

Autumn
(September–November)

As the water temperature drops below the critical 50°F (10°C) mark, the fish will stop feeding and retreat to the lower layers of the pond. You should therefore stop feeding them.

Remove all wilting or dead plant material before the winter, and put wire netting over the pond to stop leaves blowing into it. The less plant material you leave in the pond over the winter, the healthier the water will be in the spring.

If you wish, you could clean out the pond completely at this stage. Do remember, though, that many floating plants will have retreated to the pond bed in their winter form: these must be left in peace. And don't forget to remove all electric pumps and frost-sensitive plants for the winter.

Many ornamental grasses and plants (such as water plantains) look even more interesting and attractive in frost or snow, so you may want to leave them in the pond all the way through until March.

Ten basic rules for ponds

1 Don't expose your pond to uninterrupted sunlight or to complete shade.
2 Deep ponds heat up less quickly, so they're less liable to have problems in the summer. A pond with only plants and vegetation in it should measure at least 16-20 inches (40-50 cm) from the pond bed to the surface. A fish pond will need 32-36 inches (80-90 cm).
3 Ponds thrive better in a remote part of the garden that remains quiet and undisturbed. On the other hand, a pond near the house gives more pleasure to the people who live there.
4 Make sure your pond is accessible from several directions.
5 Steeply sloping banks are less good for plants or wild animals than shallow or shelved margins.
6 The bare edges of a pond liner or preformed pond don't look very attractive. If you cover them with straw or jute sacking, you can eventually disguise them with growing vegetation — and it's never too late to do this.
7 Run the lining up vertically at the edges to prevent the water being sucked out of the pond.
8 Keep algae at bay by installing plenty of floating and underwater plants, which deprive them of nutrients and light. Treat algae with chemicals only as a last resort.
9 A pond can never be too big. Don't overload it with plants: keep at least a third of the water surface free.
10 Continuous spray from fountains isn't good for some water plants — waterlilies in particular. So keep fountains well away from such plants.

Voles can do a lot of harm to a pond by gnawing through the lining. The best way to prevent this is to lay plastic-covered wire netting beneath the liner. Make sure the wire isn't too thin. Fencing wire is usually adequate. If vole damage has already occurred, use an earthenware bung to seal off the hole.

This water garden looks extremely elegant thanks to the tasteful addition of a bridge.

Index